D1764811

700000003 37 3 23

All About

PLANET
EARTH

*Investigate the amazing story
of how our world was formed*

John Farndon
CONSULTANT Rodney Walshaw

southwater

This edition is published by Southwater

Distributed in the UK by
The Manning Partnership
251–253 London Road East
Batheaston
Bath BA1 7RL
tel. 01225 852 727
fax 01225 852 852

Published in the USA by
Anness Publishing Inc.
27 West 20th Street
Suite 504
New York
NY 10011
fax 212 807 6813

Distributed in Canada by
General Publishing
895 Don Mills Road
400–402 Park Centre
Toronto, Ontario M3C 1W3
tel. 416 445 3333
fax 416 445 5991

Distributed in Australia by
Sandstone Publishing
Unit 1, 360 Norton Street
Leichhardt
New South Wales 2040
tel. 02 9560 7888
fax 02 9560 7488

Southwater is an imprint of Anness Publishing Limited
Hermes House, 88–89 Blackfriars Road, London SE1 8HA
tel. 020 7401 2077; fax 020 7633 9499

© Anness Publishing Limited 2000, 2002

Publisher: Joanna Lorenz
Managing Editor, Children's Books: Gilly Cameron Cooper
Assistant Editors: Jenni Rainford and Molly Perham
Consultant: Rodney Walshaw
Designer: Margaret Sadler
Photographer: Paul Bricknell
Stylist: Jane Coney
Picture Researcher: Caroline Brooke
Illustrators: Peter Bull Art Studio

Previously published as *Investigations: Planet Earth*

1 3 5 7 9 10 8 6 4 2

PICTURE CREDITS
b= bottom, t= top, c= centre, l= left, r= right
BBC: pages 15 tl, 18 c, 24 tr, 26 br, 31 c & bl, 33 c (also page 40 tr),
37 t & c, 39 t & b,47 t & c, 52 tl + 1 re-used in glossary; Bruce Coleman
Collection: 21 br, 30 br, 49 c, 52 c, 59 tr; Corbis: 13 bl, 16 tl, 17 c, 49 t,
50 tl, 52 c +1 re-used in glossary; Sylvia Cordaly: 45 c; Ecoscene: 22 c;
Genesis: 5 tl, 12 br; NHPA: 15 t, 21tl, 23 t, 26 tr, 27 c, 32 tl, 39 c, 41 c,
48 tl, 51 c, 53 c, 54 t, 56 tr, 57c; Oxford Scientific Films: 19 t, 52 b; Papilio
Photographic: 23 bl, 55 c, 58 c, 7 b; Planet Earth Pictures: 4 c, 4 tl, 5 cr, 8 tl,
9 br, 13 c, 16 c, 16 bl, 17 t, 20 br, 22 tl & br, 27 c, 30 tr, 31 t, 34 tl & c,
35 tr & c & br, 36 tl & br, 37 bl, 38 tr & br, 42 tl, 43 tr & br, 46 tr & c,
53 c, 54 b, 58 c & b, 59 tl; Science Photo Library: 14 t, 48 cl & cr, 59 c;
Skyscan: 13 br; Tony Stone: 9 t, 10 tl, 13 t, 15 c, 17 bl, 28 tr, 35 tl, 43 tl, 47b.

The publishers would like to thank the following children for
modelling in this book:
Emma Beardmore, Joshua Cooper, Joe Davis, Daniel Payne,
Kristy Saxena, Georgina Thomas and all the children and staff
of Hampden Gurney School.

All About
PLANET EARTH

CONTENTS

THE UNIQUE PLANET

THE EARTH is the third planet out from the Sun, the third of the nine planets that make up the solar system. It is a big round ball of rock with a metal core, wrapped in a thin blanket of colorless gases called the atmosphere. From a distance, Earth shimmers like a blue jewel in the darkness of space, because more than 70 percent of its surface is covered with water. No other planet has this much water on its surface. Jupiter's moon Europa is the only other place with much water, but it is so far away from the Sun that the water is frozen. Earth is neither too near the Sun that water is turned to steam, nor too far that it freezes. Only at the poles, is water permanently frozen in ice caps. In places, rock sticks up above the ocean waters to form half a dozen large continents and thousands of smaller islands.

Round Earth

In the last 40 years, spacecrafts have been able to take photographs of Earth from space, so we can see that it is round. The Ancient Greeks suspected that the Earth was round 2,500 years ago, because they saw how ships gradually disappeared over the horizon. But for 2,000 years, many people continued to believe that it was flat. Only when the ship of explorer Ferdinand Magellan sailed around the Earth in 1522 were people finally convinced.

Water world

An island in the Indian Ocean demonstrates all that is unique about planet Earth. The combination of vegetable and plant life, land and sea is found only on Earth—it exists nowhere else in the known universe. Life on Earth exists because it is a watery planet. Water is still, however, a precious resource. Almost 97 percent is salt water in the oceans, and three-quarters of the remaining fresh water is frozen.

The solar system

Earth's nearest companions in space are the planets Venus and Mars, all of which are much the same size. Tiny Mercury nearest the Sun, and even tinier Pluto farthest away, are the terrestrial (rocky) planets of the solar system. The other four planets—Jupiter, Saturn, Uranus and Neptune—are gigantic by comparison and are made not of rock, but gas. It was once thought the solar system was unique in the universe, but astronomers have spotted planets circling distant stars. So there may be another Earth out there after all.

Mercury

Venus

Earth

Mars

The Sun

Man on the Moon

On July 20, 1969, the American astronaut Neil Armstrong stepped from the landing module of the *Apollo 11* spacecraft onto the Moon's surface. It was the first time that a human had ever set foot on the moon. It was an exciting experience, and it reminded the astronaut just how special the Earth is. The Moon is really very close to us in space, yet it is completely lifeless, a desert of rock with no atmosphere to protect it from the Sun's dangerous rays and no water to sustain life.

The surface of Mars

Mars is similar to Earth in size, so people hoped it might have life of its own. Astronomers were once convinced that marks on the surface were canals built by Martians. Sadly, space probes to Mars have found no verifiable signs of life. As this photo from the *Pathfinder* mission shows, it is nothing but rocks and dust. But a few years ago, NASA scientists found what could be a fossil of a microscopic organism in a rock that fell from Mars.

Jupiter

Saturn

Uranus

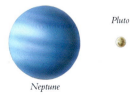

Pluto

Neptune

SPINNING PLANET

You will need: felt-tipped pen, plastic ball, piece of thin string, modeling clay, flashlight.

T HE EARTH is like a giant ball spinning in the darkness of space. The only light falling on it is the light of the Sun glowing 93 million miles away. As it spins, the Earth also moves around the Sun. The two ways of moving explain why night and day, and the seasons, occur. At any one time half the world is facing the Sun and is brightly lit, while the other half is facing away and is in darkness. As the Earth spins on its axis, the dark and sunlit halves move around, bringing night and day to different parts of the world.

The Earth is always tilted in the same direction. So when the Earth is on one side of the Sun, the Northern Hemisphere (the area north of the equator) is tilted towards the Sun, bringing summer. At this time, the Southern Hemisphere (the area south of the equator) is tilted away, bringing winter. When the Earth is on the other side of the Sun, the Northern Hemisphere is tilted away, bringing winter, while the south is in summertime. In between, as the Earth moves around to the other side of the Sun, neither hemisphere is tilted more than the other one toward the Sun. This is when spring and autumn occur. These two experiments show how this happens. The ball represents the Earth and the flashlight is the Sun.

NIGHT AND DAY

1 Draw, or cut out and glue, a shape on the ball to represent the country you live in. Stick the string to the ball with modeling clay. Tie the string to a rail or bar, such as a towel bar, so that the ball hangs freely.

2 Shine the flashlight on the ball. If your country is on the shadow half of the ball on the far side, then it is night because it is facing away from the Sun.

3 Your home country may be on the half of the ball lit by the flashlight instead. If so, it must be daytime because it is facing the Sun. Keep the flashlight level, aimed at the middle.

4 Turn the ball from left to right. As you turn the ball, the light and dark halves move around. You can see how the Sun comes up and goes down as the Earth turns.

THE SEASONS

You will need: felt-tipped pen, plastic ball, bowl just big enough for the ball to sit on, flashlight, books or a box to set the flashlight on.

1 Use the felt-tipped pen to draw a line around the middle of the ball. This represents the equator. Sit the ball on top of the bowl so that the equator line is sloping gently.

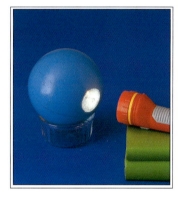

2 Put the flashlight on the books so it shines just above the equator. It is summertime on the half of the ball above the equator where the flashlight is shining, and winter in the other half of the world.

3 Shine the flashlight on the equator, as shown. It sheds an equal amount of light in each hemisphere. This is the equivalent of spring and autumn, when days and nights are of similar length throughout the world.

Half Moon

The Moon shines not because it gives out light itself but because it reflects the light of the Sun. Just as half of the Earth is always lit by the Sun, so is the other half by the Moon. The Moon appears to change shape during the month, from a crescent to a disk and back again. This is because it moves around the Earth and so we see its sunlit side from different angles. When we see a full Moon, we are seeing all of the sunlit side. The Sun and stars are our only sources of light from space.

EARTH STORY

THE SOLAR system formed 4,570 million years ago from debris left over from the explosion of a giant star. As the star debris spun around the newly formed Sun, it began to congeal into balls of dust. Quickly, the dust clumped into tiny balls of rock called planetesimals, and the planetesimals clumped together to form planets such as the Earth and Mars. At first, the Earth was little more than a ball of molten rock. Then, when the Earth was about 50 million years old, it is thought that a giant rock cannoned into it with such force that the rock melted. The melted rock cooled to become the Moon. The Earth itself was changed forever. The shock of the impact made iron and nickel collapse to Earth's center, forming a core so dense that atoms fuse in nuclear reactions. These reactions have kept the Earth's center ferociously hot ever since. The molten rock formed a thick mantle around the core, kept slowly churning by the heat.

A volcanic landscape
It is hard to imagine what the Earth's surface was like in the very early days, but you could get a good idea by staring down into the mouth of an active volcano. The collision of rocks that actually created the Earth left it incredibly hot—hot enough to melt the rock it was made from. The whole planet was just one giant, seething red hot ball of magma (molten rock).

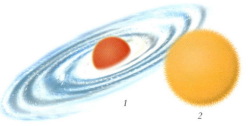

1

2

3

4

The formation of planet Earth
The solar system and planet Earth formed when gravity began to pull the debris left over from a giant star explosion into clumps (1). At first, Earth was just a molten ball, and for half a billion years it was bombarded by meteorites (2, 3). By 3.8 billion years ago, things were calming down (4, 5). The crust and atmosphere had formed, and very solid lumps of rock on the planet's surface were forming the first continents (6).

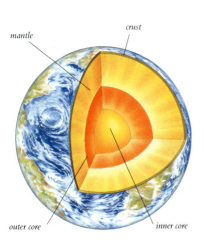

mantle

crust

outer core

inner core

The layers of the Earth
The Earth is not a solid ball of rock. The collision with the giant rock that formed the Moon caused the Earth to separate into several distinct layers. On the outside is a thin layer of solid rock, up to 25 mi. thick, called the crust. Below the crust is a thick layer of soft, semi-molten rock known as the mantle. At the center is a core of iron and nickel. The outer core is so hot it is molten, but the pressure in the inner core is so intense it cannot melt, even though temperatures here reach about 6,700°F.

5

6

Steam power

These hot springs in Iceland are sending out jets of steam heated by the Earth's interior. But they are tiny compared to the huge amounts of steam and gas that must have billowed out from the hot Earth in its early days. Two hundred million years after the birth of planet Earth, volcanic fumes formed the atmosphere. All that was missing was oxygen—the vital ingredient added later by plants.

Auroras

The spinning of the Earth swirls the iron in its core, turning it into a huge electric dynamo—and the electricity turns the Earth into a magnet. The effect of Earth's magnetism is felt tens of thousands of miles out in space. Indeed, there is a giant cocoon of magnetism around the Earth called the magnetosphere. This shields us from harmful electrically charged particles streaming from the Sun. There are small gaps in this shield above the poles. Here, charged particles collide with the atmosphere and light up the sky in spectacular displays of light called auroras.

MAGNETIC EARTH

The sailor's guide
Until the age of satellites, the magnetic compass was the sailor's main tool for finding their way at sea —working in any weather, at any time of day and on a rolling ship.

MAKE A COMPASS

You will need: bar magnet, steel needle, slice of cork, tape, small bowl, pitcher of water.

T HE EARTH behaves as if there is a giant iron bar magnet running through its middle from pole to pole. This affects every magnetic material that comes within reach. If you hold a magnet so that it can rotate freely, it always ends up pointing the same way, with one end pointing to the Earth's North Pole and the other to the South Pole. This is how a compass works—the needle automatically swings to the north. These projects show

1 To turn the needle into a magnet, stroke the end of the magnet slowly along it. Repeat this in the same direction for about 45 seconds. This magnetizes the needle.

you how to make a compass, and how you can use it to plot the Earth's magnetic field. The Earth's magnetic field is slightly tilted, so compasses do not swing to the Earth's true North Pole, but to a point that is a little way off northern Canada. This direction is known as magnetic north.

The Earth's magnetism comes from its inner core of iron and nickel. Because the outer core of the Earth is liquid and the inner core solid, the two layers rotate at different rates. This sets up circulating currents and turns it into a giant dynamo of electrical energy.

2 Place the magnetized needle on the piece of cork. Make sure that it is exactly in the middle, otherwise it will not spin evenly. Tape the needle into position.

3 Fill the bowl nearly to the top with water and float the cork in it. Make sure the cork is exactly in the middle and turns without rubbing on the edges of the bowl.

4 The Earth's magnetic field should now swivel the needle on the cork. One end of the needle will always point to the north. That end is its north pole.

MAGNETIC FIELD

You will need: *large sheet of paper, bar magnet, your needle compass from the first project, pencil.*

1 Lay a large sheet of paper on a table. Put the magnet in the middle of the paper. Set up your needle compass an inch away from one end of the magnet.

2 Wait as the compass needle settles in a particular direction as it is swiveled by the magnet. Make a pencil mark on the paper to show which way it is pointing.

3 Move the compass a little way toward the other end of the magnet. Mark a line on the paper to show which way the needle is pointing now.

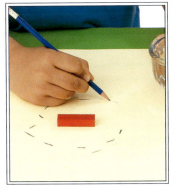

4 Repeat Step 3 for about 25 different positions around the magnet. Try the compass both near the magnet and further away. You should now have a pattern of marks.

5 Look at the pattern of marks you have made on the paper. They should form a series of rings around the magnet, like the layers of an onion. Earth's magnetic field is shaped like this.

Magnetic protection

A vast region of space about 38,000 mi. out from Earth is full of electrically charged particles. This area is called the magnetosphere. Without its protection, Earth would be exposed to the solar wind, a lethal stream of charged particles moving rapidly from the Sun.

tail of magnetosphere blown out by solar wind

lines of magnetic force

North Pole

South Pole

Earth

solar wind

Magnetosphere

LIFE-SUPPORT SYSTEM

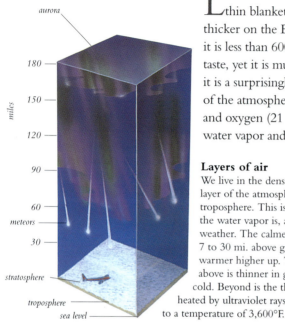

aurora

miles

180

150

120

90

60

meteors

30

stratosphere

troposphere

sea level

LIFE ON Earth exists only because of the atmosphere. This thin blanket of gases, tiny water drops and dust is barely thicker on the Earth than the skin is on an orange. At its thickest, it is less than 600 miles deep. The atmosphere has no color or taste, yet it is much more interesting than it may appear, because it is a surprisingly complex mixture of gases. Over 99 percent of the atmosphere is made up of two gases, nitrogen (78 percent) and oxygen (21 percent). It also contains argon, carbon dioxide, water vapor and minute traces of many other gases, such as helium and ozone.

Layers of air

We live in the densest, bottom layer of the atmosphere, called the troposphere. This is where most of the water vapor is, and all the weather. The calmer stratosphere is 7 to 30 mi. above ground, and gets warmer higher up. The mesosphere above is thinner in gases and very cold. Beyond is the thermosphere, heated by ultraviolet rays from the Sun to a temperature of 3,600°F.

Without the atmosphere, planet Earth would be as lifeless as the Moon. The atmosphere gives us air to breathe and water to drink, and keeps us warm. The atmosphere also acts as a shield, filtering out the Sun's harmful rays and protecting us from falling meteorites.

FACT BOX

• If all the water vapor in the air suddenly condensed, it would make the oceans 1 in. deeper.

• Over a billion tons of salt join the atmosphere from sea spray each year, and over a quarter of a billion tons of soil dust.

• The stratosphere glows faintly at night. This airglow is created by sodium or salt spray from the sea that is heated by the Sun during the day.

• Early radio signals were bounced around the world off electrically charged particles in the thermosphere.

A thin veil

Earth's atmosphere can be seen in this photograph taken from the space shuttle. The Sun is beyond the horizon, just catching the edge of the new moon high above. As the Sun's rays are scattered around, through the dense, watery, dusty lower layers of the atmosphere, they turn red and orange. Further up, where the air is thinner and there is no dust or water, the atmosphere is blue. This is what you see when you look up on a clear day. The sky is blue because gases in the air reflect mostly blue light from the Sun. Dust and moisture scatter other colors and dilute the blue.

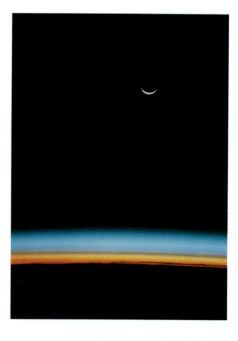

Stratocruiser

Airplanes climb high up above 7 mi. as soon as they take off. By doing this, they break out of the troposphere, where they would be buffeted by the weather, and soar into the calm stratosphere, where there is no weather at all. At this height, the passengers need to be inside a pressurized cabin. Our bodies are built to cope with the pressure of air at ground level. Up in the stratosphere where the air is thin, the pressure is too low.

Outer limits

The space shuttle orbits Earth in space about 180 mi. up. This is the outermost layer of Earth's atmosphere, the exosphere. Here the gases are rarefied; that is, they are few and far between. Above the exosphere, the atmosphere fades away into empty space. There is no oxygen at this height—just nitrogen and more of the lighter gases such as hydrogen.

Thin air

Gravity pulls most of the gases in the air into the lowest layers of the atmosphere. Seventy-five percent of the weight of the gases in the air is squashed into the troposphere, the lowest one percent of the atmosphere. The air gets thinner very quickly as you climb. Mountaineers climbing the world's highest peaks need oxygen masks to breathe because there is much less oxygen at this height.

Making clouds

Clouds are made from billions of tiny droplets of water and ice crystals so tiny that they float on the air. The droplets are formed from water vapor rising from the sea as it is warmed by the Sun. Air gets steadily colder higher up, and as the vapor rises it cools down. Eventually the water vapor gets so cold that it turns into tiny droplets of water and forms a cloud.

STIRRINGS OF LIFE

Life PROBABLY began on Earth entirely by chance, about 3.8 billion years ago. The early Earth was a hostile place. It seethed with erupting volcanoes, was washed by oceans of warm acid and enveloped in toxic fumes. But these could have been just the right conditions to start life. Amino acids, the building blocks from which the first living cells were formed, may have been created by chance as small molecules were fused together by lightning bolts that surged through the stormy air.

Recently, amazing microscopic bacteria called archaebacteria were found living on black smokers on the ocean floor, in conditions as hostile as the early Earth. It may be that bacteria such as these were the first living cells, feeding on the chemicals spewed out by volcanoes. Another kind of bacteria, called cyanobacteria, or blue-green-algae, appeared later.

Geological time

Much of what we know about the story of life on Earth comes from fossils, which are the remains of organisms in rocks. Layers of rock form one on top of each other, so the oldest is usually at the bottom, unless they have been disturbed. By studying rocks from each era, paleontologists (scientists who study fossils) have slowly built up a picture of how life has developed over millions of years.

Ancient life-form

Archaebacteria are the oldest known form of life. They seem to be able to thrive in the kind of extreme conditions that would kill almost everything else, including other bacteria. Some have been found living in boiling sulfur fumes on volcanic vents on the sea floor. This one was found in Ace Lake, Antarctica, and can survive in incredibly cold temperatures, living off carbon dioxide and hydrogen.

Hardy organisms

One of the most remarkable discoveries of recent years has been tall volcanic chimneys on the ocean floor that belch hot black smoke. These black smokers, or hydrothermal vents, are home to a community of amazing organisms that actually thrive in the scalding waters and toxic chemicals that would kill other creatures. These communities give important clues to how life could have started in the similarly hostile conditions on the primeval Earth four billion years ago.

Vast warm swamps of fern forests which form coal. First reptiles.

First insects and amphibians. Ferns and mosses as big as trees.

First land plants. Fish with jaws and freshwater fish.

Early fish-like vertebrates appear. The Sahara is glaciated.

No life on land, but shellfish flourish in the oceans.

First life-forms (bacteria) appear, and give the air oxygen.

Precambrian time

Cambrian Period 590 million years ago

Ordovician Period 505 million years ago

Silurian Period 438 million years ago

Devonian Period 408 million years ago

Carboniferou 360 million

Puffs of oxygen

Early archaebacteria left no trace. The oldest signs of life are microscopic threads in rocks dating back 3.5 billion years. The threads are like the blue-green algae called cyanobacteria that live in the oceans today. The tiny algae changed the world by using sunlight to break carbon dioxide in the air into carbon and oxygen. They fed on the carbon and expelled oxygen. The little puffs of oxygen seeped into the air, filling it with oxygen and preparing the way for life as we know it.

Ancient slime

The oldest proofs of life are stony mounds called stromatolites. Some of those at Fig Tree Rock in South Africa, date back 3.5 billion years. Stromatolites are the fossilized remains of huge colonies of slimy bacteria with a thin layer of cyanobacteria on top. The cyanobacteria obtain their food from s sunlight, while the bacteria feed on dead cyanobacteria. Stromatolites called conyphytons grew up to 300 ft high.

Clouds of life

Most scientists believe that the chemicals of life were assembled on Earth. Some, such as the late Fred Hoyle, believe life came from space. Clouds of stardust in space, called giant molecular clouds, do contain basic life chemicals. These include huge amounts of ethyl alcohol—the alcohol in drinks.

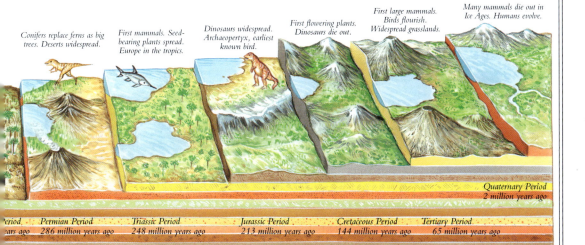

Conifers replace ferns as big trees. Deserts widespread.

First mammals. Seed-bearing plants spread. Europe in the tropics.

Dinosaurs widespread. Archaeopertyx, earliest known bird.

First flowering plants. Dinosaurs die out.

First large mammals. Birds flourish. Widespread grasslands.

Many mammals die out in Ice Ages. Humans evolve.

Quaternary Period
2 million years ago

Period.
ars ago

Permian Period
286 million years ago

Triassic Period
248 million years ago

Jurassic Period
213 million years ago

Cretaceous Period
144 million years ago

Tertiary Period
65 million years ago

EVOLUTION OF SPECIES

F OR THE first three billion years of Earth's history, the only life was in the form of microscopic, single-celled organisms in the oceans. Then, about 700 million years ago, the first real animals appeared. These were creatures such as jellyfish and sponges made from many kinds of cells, each one suited to a different task. These creatures were soft and left few traces. Over the next 100 million years, animals with shells and bones appeared. Hard parts fossilize easily, and from this time—the start of the Cambrian Period about 590 million years ago—there are very many fossils. From these, scientists have pieced together the story of how different species have come and gone. These include not only the dinosaurs, the gigantic reptiles that dominated the planet for 155 million years, but the first human-like creatures.

Ammonites
Most fossils that
are found are
shellfish, because they are
so easily preserved. One of the most
common shellfish fossils is the
ammonite, a creature a bit like a squid
that lived inside a spiral shell.
Ammonites lived in the oceans around
the time when dinosaurs dominated the
land—from 220 to 65 million years ago.
They are very common and evolved
quickly into different types, that can be
slotted into specific periods of time.
This means that geologists can use them
to date the rocks they are found in.

First plants
Life began in the oceans and moved
onto land only gradually from about
400 million years ago. The first trees
were not like today's trees. They were
the ancestors of today's ferns and
cycads, like this one in Australia.
Unlike modern trees, which grow
from seeds and flowers, ferns and
cycads grow from tiny spores. Today,
ferns and cycads are usually quite
small, but about 300 million years ago,
they grew into huge, tall forests.

Living fossils
Coelacanths are remarkable fish that first appeared 400 million years ago.
They were once thought to have died out 65 million years ago, since no
more recent fossils have been found. But in 1938 a living coelacanth was
found in the Indian Ocean. The fish have muscular, limb-like fins, and it is
from species like these that the first land creatures evolved. The limb-like fins
developed into legs so that the fish could haul themselves across mud flats.

Lifestyle

Dinosaurs dominated Earth from 225 to 65 million years ago, and then they mysteriously died out altogether. As paleontologists have found more and more dinosaur fossils, they have been able to figure out in detail what they looked like and how they lived. Stegosaurs were plant-eating dinosaurs that lived from about 180 to 80 million years ago. They had two rows of pointed plates down their back and a spiny tail that they swung to protect themselves from predators.

Frozen baby

Woolly mammoths were hairy, elephant-like creatures that lived in northern Asia and North America until about 10,000 years ago. Mammoths were probably hunted to extinction by early humans, but bodies have been found frozen in the permafrost (permanently frozen ground) of Siberia. They are so well preserved that some Japanese scientists hope to recreate them. The idea is to take from the bodies DNA, the chemical that carries their genetic code. The DNA could be used to create an embryo, which could be implanted in a living elephant.

Digging for life

When miners dig coal out of a mine, they are digging out the history of life on Earth. Coal is the fossilized remains of forests of giant club mosses and tree ferns that grew in vast tropical swamps some 350 million years ago, in the Carboniferous Period. Over millions of years, layer upon layer of dead plants sank into the swamp mud. As they were buried deeper and deeper, they were squeezed dry and became hard, slowly turning to almost pure carbon. The deeper the remains were buried, the more completely they have turned to carbon. So, coal near the surface is brown. Deep down it is jet black.

COMPETITIVE GENES

You will need: medium-size bowl, spoon, 3½ oz sea salt, liquid fish food, brine shrimp eggs from a pet store, magnifying glass.

COMPETING FOR LIFE

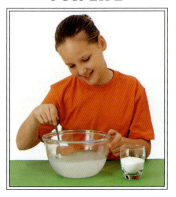

Today, there is an astonishing variety of life on Earth, with millions of species of animals and plants. Yet each one has its own natural home or way of life. Every living thing is adapted (suited) to its surroundings. In 1859, the English naturalist Charles Darwin explained all this with his theory of evolution by natural selection. This theory shows how over millions of years species gradually change or evolve. As they change, they adapt to their surroundings, and new species emerge. Evolution like this depends on the fact that no two living things are alike. So some may start life with features that make them better able to survive, as the first experiment shows. An animal, say, might have long legs to help it escape from predators. Individuals with such valuable features have a better chance of surviving. They may also have offspring that inherit these features, as in the way shown in the Strong Genes experiment. Slowly, over generations, better adapted animals and plants flourish, while others die out or find a new home. In this way, species gradually evolve.

Non-survivor
The ancient stingray fossilized here survived for millions of years. Then, this ancient species suddenly became extinct. Conditions, such as the climate, changed, and the fish did not adapt to the new conditions fast enough to survive.

1 To see how some eggs survive and others don't, pour ⅓ gallon of warm water into a bowl. Stir in the sea salt until it dissolves. When the water is cool, add a few drops of fish food.

2 Sprinkle in a spoonful of shrimp eggs. Set the bowl in a warm place so that the water will stay at 70°F.

3 After a few days, some shrimps will hatch into larvae. Stir the water once a day and scoop out a spoonful. Be careful not to disturb the larvae too much.

4 Using a magnifying glass, count how many eggs and larvae you see on the spoon. When adults appear, count these too. Only the strongest will survive and grow into adults.

The lottery of life

Only a tiny proportion of this dragonfly's thousands of eggs will live to adulthood. Dragonflies generally have adapted well to changing conditions. They are the longest-surviving of all insect species. More than 300 million years ago, they were the first animals to fly.

STRONG GENES

You will need: pack of ordinary playing cards. This is a game for three or more players.

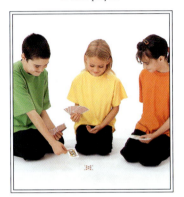

1 Deal seven cards to each player. The cards are your supply of genes for life. The suit of diamonds represents strong genes that give you a better a chance of survival.

2 Each player lays down a card in turn, following suit. If you cannot follow suit, play a diamond—a strong gene. If you play a diamond, always pick it up and save for the next deal.

3 The player who plays the highest card (or a diamond) wins the round, and begins the next. Once all the cards have been played, the player who has won the fewest rounds drops out.

4 Deal six cards to each survivor. Each player then picks up their diamonds from the previous round. Discard one card from the six for each diamond you pick up.

5 Play out all the cards in rounds as before. Again the player who wins the fewest rounds must drop out. Repeat Step 4 dealing five cards each. Play again with four cards, then three, then two, then one. The last player survives life's game.

BROKEN EARTH

THE SURFACE of the Earth is not in one piece, but cracked like a broken eggshell, into 20 or so giant slabs. The giant slabs, called tectonic plates, are huge, thin pieces of rock thousands of miles across but often little more than a dozen miles thick. The plates are not set in one place, but are slipping and sliding around the Earth all the time. They move very slowly—at about the pace of a fingernail growing—but they are so gigantic their movement has dramatic effects on the Earth's surface. The movement of the plates causes earthquakes, pushes up volcanoes and mountains and makes the continents move. Once, the continents were all joined together in one huge continent that geologists call Pangea, surrounded by a giant ocean called Panthalassa. About 200 million years ago the plates beneath Pangea began to split up and move apart, carrying fragments of the continent with them. These fragments slowly drifted to the positions they are in now.

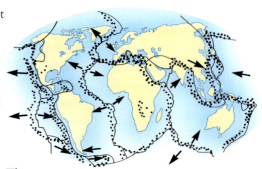

Surface sections
The Earth's rigid shell is called the lithosphere, from the Greek word *lithos* (stone). It is broken into the huge fragments shown on this map. The African plate is gigantic, underlying not only Africa but half of the Atlantic Ocean too. The Cocos plate under the West Indies is quite small. Black dots mark the origins of major earthquakes over a year. Note how they coincide with the plate margins.

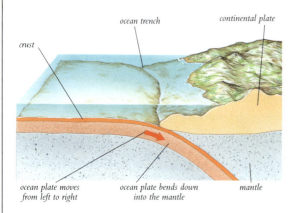

crust

ocean trench

continental plate

ocean plate moves from left to right

ocean plate bends down into the mantle

mantle

Plates in collision
In many places, tectonic plates are slowly crunching together with enormous force. As they collide, one plate may be forced under the other in a process called subduction, which means drawing under. The plate is completely destroyed as the plate slides down into the heat of the Earth's mantle. Earthquakes are often generated as it slides down, and the melting rock bubbles up as violent volcanoes. Subduction zones occur right around the western edge of the Pacific Ocean.

Lowest place on Earth
When one plate is forced down beneath another, it can open up deep trenches in the ocean floor. These trenches are the lowest places on the Earth's surface. They plunge so far down that the water is darker than the blackest night. These dark abysses have been never been fully explored, but this photograph was taken at the bottom of the world's deepest trench, the Marianas Trench, at a depth of over 32,000 ft.

Two-way friction

In some places, the plates are neither crunching together nor pulling apart. Instead, they are shaking sideways past each other. This is happening at the San Andreas fault in California. The giant Pacific plate is sliding at a rate of 2½ in. a year northwest past the North American plate. This has set off earthquakes that have rocked the cities of San Francisco and Los Angeles.

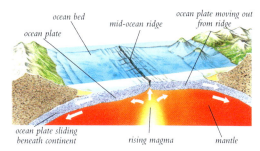

ocean bed • mid-ocean ridge • ocean plate moving out from ridge • ocean plate • ocean plate sliding beneath continent • rising magma • mantle

Mid-ocean ridge

Right down the middle of the sea bed in the Atlantic Ocean, there is a giant crack where the tectonic plates are pulling apart. Here, molten rock from the Earth's interior wells up into the crack and freezes onto the edges of the plates. This creates a series of jagged ridges called the mid-ocean ridge. As the plates move apart and new rock is added on the edges, so the sea floor spreads wider.

A string of islands

As one colliding plate is forced down beneath another into the Earth's hot interior, it melts. The melting rock is squeezed into cracks in the overlying plate and bursts onto the surface as a line of volcanoes. If this line is in the sea, the volcanoes form a long, curving string of islands called an island arc. Many of the islands in the western Pacific formed in this way.

FACT BOX

• The west coast of Africa looks as though it would slot into the east coast of South America because they were once joined together.

• New York is moving ¾-1¼ in. away from London every year.

BUILDING MOUNTAINS

Lone volcano
Mount Kilimanjaro, on the border of Kenya and Tanzania, is Africa's highest mountain, reaching 19,340 ft. This distinctive volcanic cone rises in isolated majesty from the surrounding grassland. It was formed where a rising plume of hot rock in the Earth's interior burned its way up through the tectonic plate that underlies East Africa. Mount Kilimanjaro is high enough to be snowcapped, even though it lies near the equator.

A FEW of the world's highest mountains, such as Mount Kilimanjaro in Africa, are lone volcanoes, built up by successive eruptions. Most high mountains are part of great ranges that stretch for hundreds of miles. Mountains look as though they have been there forever, but geologically they are quite young. They have all been created in the last couple of hundred million years—the last quarter of the world's history—by the huge power of the Earth's crust as it moves. The biggest ranges, such as the Himalayas and the Andes, are fold mountains. These are great piles of crumpled rock pushed up by the collision of two of the great plates that make up the Earth's surface. Folding opens up many cracks in the rock and the weather attacks them, etching the mountains into jagged peaks and knife-edge ridges. Some mountain ranges, in the central parts of plates, are huge blocks of the Earth's crust that have been pushed up as the plate was stretched.

Bow-wave
Geologists used to think that rock crumples to form fold mountains, such as the Alps, in rigid layers. Now they are beginning to think that because this all happens so slowly, the rock flows almost like very thick molasses. They suggest that as one tectonic plate collides with another, the rock is pushed up like the v-shaped bow-wave in front of a boat. Like a very slow bow-wave, the mountains are continually piling up in front of the plate and flowing away at the side.

Continental crunch
The incredible contortions created by rock folding even on a small scale are clearly visible in the zigzag layers of shale. These rocks in Devon, England were folded about 250 million years ago. This was when a mighty collision between two continents that formed the single giant continent of Pangea. Present-day Devon was one of the places that was squeezed in the gap.

Waves in the Andes
Using the latest satellite techniques, geologists have surveyed many of the world's high mountain ranges, including the Andes, the Himalayas, the European Alps and New Zealand. What they have found is something remarkable. When compared to surveys from a century ago, mountain peaks in these ranges have moved exactly as though they are flowing very slowly. So the folds in the rock you see in this photograph may not be folds but very, very slow and stiff waves.

How faults occur

The slow, unstoppable movement of tectonic plates puts rock under such huge stress that it sometimes cracks. Such cracks are called faults. Where they occur, huge blocks of rock slip up and down past each other, creating cliffs. In places a whole series of giant blocks may be thrown up together, creating a new mountain range. The Black Mountains in Germany are an example of block mountains formed in this way.

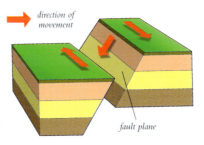

direction of movement

fault plane

The Earth splits open

The Great Rift Valley runs for more than 1,800 mi. down the east of Africa from the Red Sea. The movement of the Earth's tectonic plates not only builds up mountains, it also opens up great valleys. Where plates are pulling apart, or magma is pushing up underneath, the land can split like the crust of a pie in the oven. Land can drop along this crack to form a rift valley.

Zagros Mountains, Iran

For the last 100 million years, the tectonic plates carrying Africa and Arabia have been plowing northward into Eurasia. The tremendous impact has crumpled the edge of Eurasia and thrown up a belt of mountains stretching all the way from southern Europe, through the Aegean and Turkey to the Zagros Mountains of Iran. The Turkish and Iranian end remains very active, building up the mountains still higher, and setting off earthquakes.

FOLDING TECHNIQUES

ROCKS TEND to form in flat layers called strata. Some, called sedimentary rocks, form when sand and gravel and seashells settle on the sea bed. Volcanic rocks form as hot molten rock streams from volcanoes that flood across the landscape.

Although rock layers may be flat to begin with, they do not always stay that way. Most of the great mountain ranges of the world began as flat layers of rock that crumpled. They were crumpled by the slow but immensely powerful movement of the great tectonic plates that make up the Earth's surface. Mountains occur mostly where the plates are crunching together, pushing up the rock layers along their edges into massive folds. These two experiments help you to understand just how that happens. Sometimes, the folds can be tiny wrinkles just an inch or so long in the surface of a rock. Sometimes, they are gigantic, with hundreds of miles between the crests of each fold. As the layers of rock are squeezed horizontally, they become more and more folded. Some folds turn right over to form overlapping folds called nappes. As nappes fold upon each other, the crumpled layers of rock are raised progressively higher to form mountains. Sometimes you can see the complicated twists of folds on the side of a mountain or cliff.

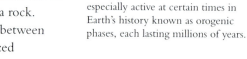

Mountain range
Although many mountain ranges are getting higher at this very moment as plates move together, mountain building is thought to have been especially active at certain times in Earth's history known as orogenic phases, each lasting millions of years.

SIMPLE FOLDS
You will need: thin rug.

1 Find an uncarpeted floor and lay the rug with the short, straight edge up against a wall. Make sure the long edge of the rug is at a right angle to the wall.

2 Now push the outer edge of the rug toward the wall. See how the rug crumples. This is how rock layers buckle to form mountains as tectonic plates push against each other.

3 Push the rug up against the wall even more and you will see some of the folds turn right over on top of each other. These are folded-over strata or layers, called nappes.

COMPLEX FOLDS

You will need: rolling pin, different colors of modeling clay, modeling tool, two blocks of wood measuring 2-in. square, two bars of wood measuring 4 x 2 in.

1 Roll out the modeling clay into flat sheets, each about ¼ in. thick. Cut the clay into strips about same width as the blocks of wood. Square off the ends.

2 Lay the plasticine strips carefully one on top of the other, in alternating colors or series of colors. These strips represent the layers of rock.

Features of a fold

Geologists describe an upfold as an anticline and a downfold as a syncline. The dip is the direction the fold is sloping. The angle of dip is how steep the slope is. The strike is the line along the fold. The axial plane is an imaginary line through the center of the fold—this may be vertical, horizontal or at any angle in between.

3 Place the blocks of wood at both ends of the strips of plasticine. Lay the bars of wood down both sides of the strips to stop them from twisting sideways.

5 Occasionally, stop and pull away the bars of wood to see what is happening. As you push harder, see how the layers crumple increasingly.

4 Ask a friend to hold on to one block while you push the other towards it. As you push, the effect is similar to two tectonic plates slowly pushing together.

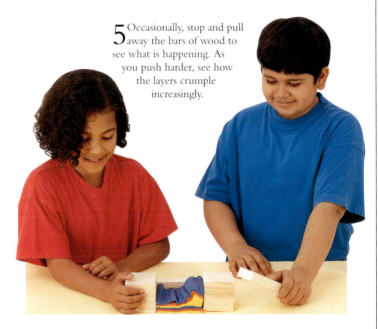

WEARING AWAY

IF YOU went to the Moon, you would see the footprints of the first astronauts to set foot there way back in 1969. They are still there because the Moon's surface never changes. It has no atmosphere and its surface is now completely still. Earth's surface changes all the time. Most of these changes take place over millions of years, far too gradually for us to see. Occasionally, though, the landscape is reshaped dramatically and quickly, such as when a volcano throws up a completely new mountain in minutes, or an avalanche brings down the entire side of a hill in seconds. The Earth's surface is shaped in two ways. First, it is distorted and reformed from below by the gigantic forces of the Earth's interior. Second, it is shaped from above by the weather, running water, waves, moving ice, wind and other agents of erosion.

The mountain's end

In mountainous regions, the attack of the weather on rock can break off huge amounts of debris. Millions of years of shattering, especially by frost, can create vast numbers of angular stones called "scree." As the stones fall off steep slopes, they gather at the foot of the slope in huge piles called scree slopes. Eventually, these stones will be broken down. They will form fine sand and silt and gradually wash away down to the sea where they can begin to form new rock.

Cycle of erosion

A century ago, Harvard Professor W. M. Davis (1850–1935) suggested that landscapes are shaped by "cycles of erosion" going through "youth, maturity and old age." This theory gave an idea of how landscapes evolve, but research has shown that the truth is more complex.

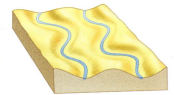

Youth: After an uplift of the land, there is vigorous erosion as fast-flowing streams bite deep into the landscape.

Maturity: River valleys get wider and slopes get gentler as they are worn away. Hill tops are rounded off.

Old age: Valleys are worn flat into wide plains called peneplains and slopes are reduced to isolated hills.

Shattered peaks

As soon as rock is exposed to the weather, it starts to break down under the assault of wind and rain, frost and sunlight. Sometimes the rock is corroded (eaten away) by chemicals in the air, or rainwater trickling over it. Sometimes it is broken down physically by, for example, the effects of heat and cold. Water in cracks can expand so forcefully as it freezes that it can shatter the toughest rock.

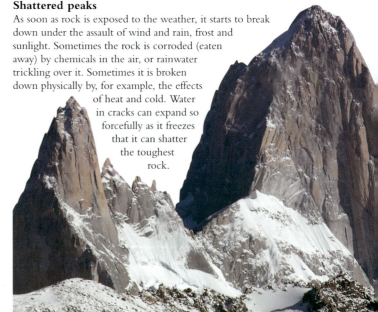

Tors and kopjes

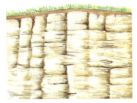

Water trickles down into the ground through joints and cracks in the rock.

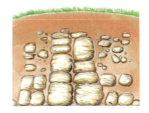

The water corrodes and widens the joints, and the soft debris is washed away.

Eventually, only the big, intact blocks are left perched on the hill top.

In cool regions, there are outcrops called tors on the tops of moors. What is surprising about tors is that they are made from massive blocks that poke above completely smooth slopes, like a castle on a hilltop. There are similar outcrops called kopjes in the tropics. Both features are thought to have been created by the gradual uncovering of rock that has been corroded into big blocks by chemicals in water trickling through the ground, as the pictures above show.

Desert sculpture

In most places, running water is the main agent of erosion. The landscape is molded into rounded hills and deep valleys by the wash of rivers and streams. In deserts, however, running water is sparse, although rivers may flow for a short time after rain and cut valleys. Much of the landscape is sharp and angular and cut into weird shapes by the blast of windblown sand. This is Mexican Hat in the Utah Desert in North America.

FACT BOX

• At -7.6°F, ice can exert a pressure of 6,600 lbs on an area the size of a coin.

• The Colorado River began carving out the Grand Canyon 60 million years ago, as the river plain was slowly uplifted by giant movements of the Earth's crust, forming a plateau.

Acid work

A limestone statue on Gloucester Cathedral in England has worn away. Some rocks are better than others for building materials. All rain is slightly acidic. Limestone rock is especially susceptible to corrosion by acidic rainwater. The rainwater seeps into cracks in the rock, eating it away underground and creating potholes, tunnels and spectacular caverns.

PRACTICAL EROSION

Rocks and mountains look tough, but all the time they are being worn away by the weather, by running water, by waves, by glaciers and by the wind. It is such a slow process that you can rarely see it happening. These three projects speed up the process so that you can see instantly what takes millions of years in nature. The landscape is slowly reshaped, as rocks crumble and mountains are worn down in a process called denudation (laying bare). Much of the damage is done by the weather.

Wherever rock is exposed to the weather, it is attacked by the atmosphere and begins to crumble away. This process is called weathering. Mechanical weathering is when rock is broken down by heat and cold. In areas where the temperature falls below freezing, water seeps into cracks in rocks and then freezes. It expands as it freezes, making the rock shatter or split. Chemical weathering is when the slight acidity of rainwater dissolves rock like tea dissolving sugar. Limestone landscapes can be corroded into fantastic shapes by chemical weathering.

Eroded landscape
Often, the effects of denudation are hidden under a covering of soil and debris. But they are obvious here in this dry landscape where the damage done by the weather and water running off the land is clearly exposed.

THE DESTRUCTIVE POWER OF WATER

You will need: baking sheet, brick, tray or bowl, sand, castle mold, pitcher, water.

1 Put one end of a baking sheet on a brick. Put the other end of the baking sheet on a lower tray or bowl, so that it slopes downward. Make a sandcastle on the baking sheet.

2 Slowly drip water on the castle. Watch the sand crumble and form a new shape. This is because the sand erodes away where the water hits it.

3 Ensure that the water flows down the center of the baking sheet. This way the water hits the middle of the sand castle, eroding the center to form a natural stack.

HARD WATER

You will need: *3 small aluminum foil sheets or saucers, pitcher, mineral water, tap water, distilled water, 3 labels, pen.*

1 Fill three foil sheets or saucers with a small amount of water—one with mineral water, one with tap water and one with distilled water.

2 Label the sheets with the type of water in them and set them somewhere warm and well-ventilated. Ensure that they will not be disturbed for a few days.

3 Examine the sheets once the water has evaporated. You will see that the distilled water has not deposited minerals because it does not contain any. Mineral water deposits only a few minerals. Tap water deposits vary depending on where you live. In hard water areas, tap water flows over rocks such as limestone and chalk, and deposits lime minerals. Water in soft water areas flows over rocks such as sandstone. This does not dissolve in water and leave a deposit.

distilled water

tap water

mineral water

CHEMICAL EROSION

You will need: *baking sheet, brown sugar, pitcher of water.*

1 Build a pile of brown sugar on a sheet. Imagine that it is a mountain made of a soluble rock (dissolves in water). Press the sugar down firmly and shape it to a point.

2 Drip water on your sugar mountain. It will erode as the water dissolves the sugar. The water running off should be brown, because it contains dissolved brown sugar.

RUNNING RIVERS

IVERS PLAY a large part in shaping the landscape. Without them, the landscapes would be as rough and jagged as the surface of the Moon. Tumbling streams and broad rivers gradually mold and soften contours, wearing away material and depositing it elsewhere. Over millions of years, a river can carve a gorge thousands of yards deep through solid rock, or spread out a vast plain of fine silt. Wherever there is water to sustain them, rivers flow across the landscape. They start high in the hills and wind their way down toward the sea or a lake. At its head, a river is little more than a trickle, a tiny stream tumbling down the mountain slopes. It is formed by rain running off the mountainside or by water bubbling up from a spring. As the river flows downhill, it is joined by more and more tributaries and gradually grows bigger. As it grows, its nature as well as its power change dramatically.

Thundering water

Waterfalls are found where a river plunges straight over a rock ledge and drops vertically. Typically, they occur where the river flows across a band of hard rock. The river wears away the soft material beyond the hard rock and makes a sudden step down. This is Victoria Falls in Zimbabwe, formed where the Zambezi River suddenly drops about 300 ft into a deep, narrow chasm. The spray and the roar of the water have given the Falls the local name *Mosi oa Tunya,* the smoke that thunders.

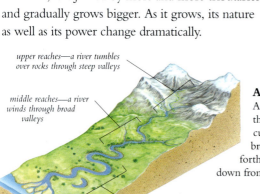

upper reaches—a river tumbles over rocks through steep valleys

middle reaches—a river winds through broad valleys

lower reaches—a river winds broad and smooth across flat floodplains

A river's course

As it flows down to the sea, a river changes its character. In the upper reaches, it is a fast-flowing, tumbling stream that cuts down through steep, narrow valleys. Lower down, a river broadens and deepens. Eventually, it meanders (winds) back and forth across broad floodplains made of material that it has washed down from higher up.

Forceful

High in the mountains, streams are small and tumble down over rocks and boulders. The valley is narrow with steep sides. Boulders often crash down into the stream bed so that the stream is forced to wind its way around them. The flow of water is very erratic. In flat places it flows slowly, whereas in other places it plunges down fast and furiously over rapids and waterfalls. Sometimes, when snow melts, the water level may rise enough to roll big boulders along.

Winding rivers

All rivers wind. As they near the sea, they wind more often, forming horseshoe-shaped bends called meanders, like these in the Guiana Highlands. Meanders begin as the river deposits sediments along its bed in ups and downs called pools (deeps) and riffles (shallows). The distance between pools and riffles, and the size of meanders, is usually in proportion to the width of the river. Meanders develop as the river cuts into the outer bank of a bend and deposits sand and mud on the inner bank.

Colorado loop

Big "gooseneck" bends usually only form when a river is crossing broad plains. But here on the Colorado, a gooseneck is in a deep gorge. A meander that cuts into a gorge in this way is called an incised meander. It probably formed millions of years ago when the Colorado Plateau was a flat lowland. The land was lifted upward and the meander cut deeper as the land rose.

Black river

The Rio Negro, a major tributary of the Amazon in South America, is inky black. This is because of the rotting vegetable matter the river has picked up from the mangrove swamps it flows through. This is why it is called the Negro—*negro* is Spanish for black. Rivers carry their load of sediment in three ways. Big stones are rolled along the river bed. Smaller grains are bounced along the bed. The finest grains float in the water. Typically the load is mostly yellowish silt (fine mud) and sand. The Yangtze River in China carries so much yellow silt that it is often known as the Yellow River.

LAYING DOWN DEPOSITS

Sluggish waters
This river is flowing so slowly, as it nears the sea, that it cannot carry debris such as sand and mud. It begins to deposit its load, forming mudbanks, low-lying islands and fan-shaped deltas.

As rock is rotted away by the weather, the fragments move downhill. The rotted rock may slip down suddenly in a lump, creating a landslide or an avalanche. Sometimes, though, the debris creeps down, bit by bit, over many years. The rocky particles mix with vegetation and may be broken down into soil by further weathering and by bacteria and other organisms. Eventually the debris reaches the bottom of a slope. It is then washed away by a river, a glacier, by waves or, if the debris is very fine and dry, blown along by the wind. Big rivers such as the Mississippi carry huge amounts of debris. Even the biggest rivers, though, can only carry so much and must sometimes deposit their load of debris along the river's course. Rivers, glaciers, waves and wind all have their own characteristic ways of depositing debris as these projects show. Rivers flood out to deposit wide plains of silt called floodplains. Glaciers drop hummocks of material called moraines. Waves create beaches. Winds pile up dust in deposits called loesses or build up sand-dunes.

HOW WIND SORTS SAND

You will need: *two empty ice cube trays, piece of cardboard large enough to fit over an ice cube tray, spoon, mix of fine and coarse sand, hairdryer.*

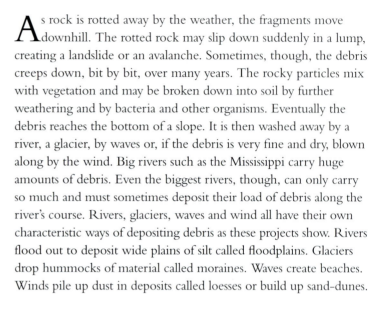

1 Turn one ice cube tray over, and lay it down end to end with another ice cube tray. Place the cardboard over the upturned tray and spoon the sand over it to make a sand dune.

2 Hold a hairdryer close to the upturned tray, pointing toward the other tray. Turn the hairdryer on so that it blows sand into the open ice cube tray.

3 Look at the grains that have fallen into each box. The distance a grain travels depends on its weight. Heavy grains fall in the end of the tray nearest to you. Light grains are blown to the farthest end

HOW WATER MAKES RIPPLES IN SAND

You will need: *heavy, filled tin can, round plastic bowl, water, fine clean sand, spoon.*

1 Place the tin can in the center of the plastic bowl, then fill the bowl, with water to at least half way. The water should not cover more than two-thirds of the tin can.

2 Sprinkle a little sand into the bowl to create a thin layer about ¼ in. deep. Spread the sand until it is even, then let it settle into a flat layer at the bottom of the bowl.

3 Stir the water gently with the spoon. Drag it in a circle around the tin can. As the water begins to swirl, stir faster, but keep it smooth.

Beach deposits

Waves often make ripples on a sandy beach like those in the project. Much of the rock debris washed down by rivers eventually ends up in the sea. Most settles slowly on the sea bed and compacts to form new sedimentary rocks. Some, though, is washed up by waves against the shore, and forms beaches.

4 As you stir faster, let the water swirl around by itself. The sand develops ripples. As you stir faster, the ripples become more defined.

33

ICE SCULPTING

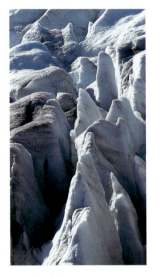

GLACIERS ARE "rivers" of slowly moving ice that form in mountain regions where it is too cold for the snow to melt. They flow down mountain valleys, creeping lower and lower until they reach a point where the ice begins to melt.

The ice in a glacier is not clear, but opaque like packed snowballs. The surface is streaked with bands of debris, such as rocks, that has fallen from the mountain slopes above. Massive cracks appear where the ice travels over bumps in the valley floor. Today, glaciers form only in high mountains and near the North and South Poles. In the past, during cold periods called Ice Ages, they were far more widespread, covering huge areas of North America and Europe. When the ice melted, dramatic marks were left on the landscape. In the mountains of northwest America and Scotland the ice gouged out giant, trough-like valleys. Over much of the American midwest and the plains of northern Europe lay vast deposits of till (rock debris).

Cracked ice

As a glacier moves downhill, it bends and stretches, opening deep cracks called crevasses. These may be covered by fresh falls of snow, making the glacier treacherous for climbers to cross. Crevasses may be a sign that the glacier is passing over a bar of rock on the valley floor. A bergschrund is a deep crevasse where the ice pulls away from the back wall of the cirque at the start of the glacier.

Old and new snow

The snow on these mountain peaks is likely to be quite different from that of the glacier below. Glaciers are made up of névé (new snow) and a compacted layer of old snow, or firn, beneath. All the air is squeezed out of the firn so that it looks like ice. The ice becomes more compacted over time, turning into thick white glacier ice, which begins to flow slowly downhill.

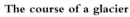

bergschrund

medial (middle) moraine

cirque

crevasses

snout

terminal (end) moraine

The course of a glacier

A glacier typically begins in a hollow high in the mountains called a cirque. It then spills out over the lip of the cirque and flows down the valley. If the underside of the glacier is "warm" (about 32°F), it glides in a big lump on a film of water melted by the pressure of ice. This is called basal slip. If the underside of the glacier is well below 32°F, it moves though there were layers within the ice slipping over each other like the shuffling of a deck of cards. This is called internal deformation. Glaciers usually move in this way high up where temperatures are lower, and by basal slip farther down.

Deep digging

The fjords of Norway were made by glaciers that carved out deep valleys well below the current sea level. When the ice retreated, sea flooded the valleys to form inlets that in places are over 3,200 ft deep. Glaciers may be slow, but their sheer weight and size gives them the immense power needed to mold the landscape. They carve out wide valleys, gouge great bowls out of mountains, and slice away entire hills and valleys as they move relentlessly on.

Moraine and drift

The gray bank across the picture above is a terminal (end) moraine. This is where debris has piled up in front of a glacier that has melted. The intense cold around a glacier causes rocks to shatter, and as the ice bulldozes through valleys, it shears huge amounts of rock from the valley walls. The glacier carries all this debris and drops it in piles called moraines. Melting glaciers deposit blankets of fine debris called glaciofluvial (ice river) drift.

Alaskan tundra

This landscape in Alaska is shaped by its periglacial climate (the climate near a glacial region). Winters are long and cold with temperatures always below freezing. In the short summers, ice melts only on the surface, and so the ground beneath is permafrost (permanently frozen). Water collects on the surface and makes the land boggy. As the ice melts, it stirs and buckles the ground beneath. As the ground thaws, then freezes again, cracks form, creating deep wedges of ice.

Glaciated valley

A wide, U–shaped valley in Scotland is left over from the Ice Ages, when glaciers were much more widespread. The last of the Ice Ages ended about 10,000 years ago. Valleys like this were carved by glaciers over tens of thousands of years. They are very different from the winding V-shape of a valley cut by a river.

DESERT LANDSCAPES

Water in the desert
A valuable pocket of moisture has formed in the desert. There is often water beneath the surface of a desert, which may be left over from wetter days in the past. It may be water from wetter regions farther away, which has run down sloping rock layers beneath the desert. Occasionally, the fierce desert wind blows a hollow out of the sand so deep that it exposes this underground water.

Not all deserts are vast seas of sand. Some are rock-strewn plains. Others are huge blocks of mountains standing alone in wide basins, or just empty expanses of ice, as in Antarctica. All have the one common characteristic of being very dry. The lack of water makes desert landscapes very different from any others. Wind plays a much more important part in shaping them, because there is neither moisture to bind things together nor running water to mold them. In the desert, wind carves many unusual and unique landforms, from sculpted rocks to moving sand dunes. Very few places in the world are entirely without water, and intermittent (occasional) floods do have a dramatic effect on many desert landscapes. Instead of the rounded contours of wetter landscapes, steep cliffs, narrow gorges and pillar-like plateaus called mesas and buttes are formed.

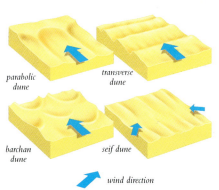

parabolic
dune

transverse
dune

barchan
dune

seif dune

wind direction

Sand dune styles
In some deserts, such as the Sahara, there are vast seas of sand, called ergs, where the wind piles sand up into dunes. The type of dune depends on the amount of sand and the wind direction. Crescent-shaped dunes called parabolic dunes are common on coasts. Ones with tails facing away from the wind are called barchans. These dunes creep slowly forward. Transverse dunes form at right angles to the main wind direction where there is lots of sand. Seifs form when there is little sand and the wind comes from different directions.

Dune sea
In the western Sahara, giant sand dunes hundreds of yards high have formed as a result of two million years of dry conditions. In places, the wind has piled up the dunes into long ridges called draa, that stretch far across the desert like giant waves in the sea. Each year, these ridges are moved 80 ft farther by the wind, as sand is blown up one side and rolls down the far side. Space probes have seen dunes like these on the planet Mars.

Monuments to water

Monument Valley in Utah, is a spectacular example of what water erosion can do in dry places. The monuments are physical features called mesas. They are protected from water erosion by a cap of hard rock. The softer, unprotected rock between them has been washed away over millions of years. As water flows in channels rather than overland, there is nothing to round the contours, and cliffs remain sheer.

Occasional rivers

Rain is rare in the desert. What rain there is flows straight off the land and does not soak in, so streams rarely flow all the time. Instead, most streams flow only every now and then, and are said to be ephemeral or intermittent. In between wet periods they leave behind dry beds called arroyos. In the Sahara Desert and the Middle East, rare rain torrents wash out narrow gorges called wadis. These are normally dry, but after rain may fill rapidly with water in a flash flood.

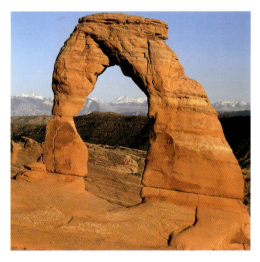

The power of the wind

Strong winds blow unobstructed across the desert, picking up grains of sand and hurling them at rocks. The sandblasting can sculpt rocks into fantastic shapes such as this rock arch. Satellite pictures have revealed parallel rows of huge, wind-sculpted ridges in the Atacama Desert in Chile and in the Sahara Desert in Africa. These are called yardangs and are hundreds of yards high and dozens of miles long.

FACT BOX

• Summer temperatures in the Sudan Desert in Africa can soar to 133°F, hotter than anywhere else in the world.

• Because desert skies are clear, heat escapes at night and temperatures can be very low.

• Not all the world's deserts are hot. Among the world's biggest deserts are the Arctic and Antarctic, both of which have hardly more rain than the Sahara.

SEA BATTLES

COASTLINES ARE constantly changing shape. They change every second, as a new wave rolls in and drops back again, and every six hours, as the tide rises and falls. Over longer periods, too, coastlines are reshaped by the continuous assault of waves. They change more rapidly than any other type of landscape. Of all the agents that erode (wear away) the land, the sea is the most powerful of all.

Huge cliffs are carved out of mountains, broad platforms are sliced back through the toughest of rocks, and houses are left dangling over the edges of the land. Such examples are proof of the awesome force of waves. The sea is not always destructive, though. It also builds. Where headland cliffs are being eroded by waves, the bays between may fill with sand—often with the same material from the headlands. On low coasts where the sea is shallow, waves build beaches and banks of shingle, sand and mud. How a coastline shapes up depends on the sort of material it is made of and on the direction and power of the waves.

White cliffs
Waves can quickly wear the land into sheer cliffs like those at Beachy Head in England. When the last Ice Age ended about 8,000 years ago, the sea level rose as the ice melted. Sea flooded over the land to form what is now the English Channel. The waves quickly began to slice away the land. The valleys were cut off so that they became just dips in the cliffline, while the hills became crests.

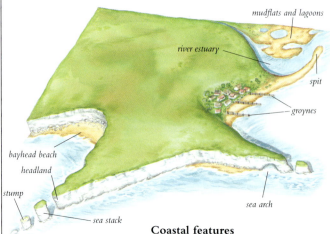

mudflats and lagoons

river estuary

spit

groynes

bayhead beach

headland

stump

sea arch

sea stack

Coastal features
The sea's power to build and destroy a coastline can be seen in this picture. Exposed parts of the coast that face into the waves are eroded into steep cliffs. Headlands are worn back, leaving behind stacks, stumps and arches. In more sheltered places, the sand piles up to form beaches, or waves may carry material along the coast to build spits and mudflats.

Saving the beach
Low fences called groynes have been built along this beach to stop it from being carried away by the wave action. When waves hit a coast at an angle, they fall back down the beach at right angles. Any sand and shingle carried by a wave falls back slightly farther along the beach. In this way, sand and shingle is carried along the beach in a zigzag movement called longshore drift.

Storm force

During a storm, the waves crash onto the shore with tremendous force. The waves attack hard rock in two ways. They pound the rock with a huge weight of water filled with stones. They also split the rock apart as the waves force air into cracks. On high coasts, the constant attack of waves undercuts the foot of the slope, and unsupported upper parts topple down to create a cliff.

Wave-cut platforms

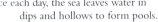

A pool has formed in a dip on a rocky platform on the seashore. The sea's erosive power is concentrated in a narrow band at the height of the waves. As the waves wear back sea cliffs, they leave the rock below wave height untouched. As the cliff retreats, the waves slice off a broad platform of rock. Geologists call this a wave-cut platform, and it lies between the low-tide and high-tide marks. As the tide goes out twice each day, the sea leaves water in dips and hollows to form pools.

Rock arch

The sea arch at Durdle Door in Dorset, England, is made by waves eating away at large blocks of well-jointed rock. The waves have worked their way into joints in the rock and slowly enlarged them. Eventually, the cracks are so big that they open up into sea caves, or cut right through the foot of a headland to create a sea arch like this. When further erosion makes the top of an arch collapse, pillars called stacks are left behind. Pillars may then be eroded into shorter stumps.

PULLING TIDES

Every 12 hours or so, the sea rises a little in some places, then falls back again. These rises and falls are called tides, and they are caused mostly by the Moon. The Moon is far away, but gravity pulls the Earth and Moon together quite strongly. The pull is enough to pull the water in the oceans into an egg shape around the Earth. This creates a bulge of water—a high tide—on each side of the world. As the Earth turns around, these bulges of water stay in the same place beneath the Moon. The effect is that they run around the world, making the tide rise and fall twice a day as each bulge passes. Actually, the continents get in the way of these tidal bulges, making the water move around in a complicated way.

The first experiment on these pages shows how the oceans can rise and fall a huge distance through tides without any change in the amount of water in the oceans at all. The second shows what the tidal bulge would look like if you could slice through the Earth, and how it moves around as the Earth turns beneath the Moon.

Low tide
The height of tides varies a great deal from place to place. In the open ocean, the water may not go up and down more than a yard or so. But in certain narrow inlets and enclosed seas, the water can bounce around until tides of 50 ft or more can build up.

HIGH AND LOW TIDE
You will need: round plastic bowl, water, big plastic ball to represent the world.

1 Place the bowl on a firm surface, then half fill it with water. Place the ball gently in the water so that it floats in the middle of the bowl.

2 Put both hands on the top of the ball, and push it down into the water gently but firmly. Look what happens to the level of water; it rises in a "high tide."

3 Let the ball gently rise again. Now you can see the water in the bowl dropping again. So the tide has risen and fallen, even though the amount of water is unchanged.

THE TIDAL BULGE

You will need: *strong glue, one 8-in. length and two 6-in. lengths of thin string, big plastic ball to represent the world, round plastic bowl, water, adult with a simple hand drill.*

1 Glue the 8-in. length of string very firmly to the ball and let dry. Ask an adult to drill two holes in the rim of the bowl on opposite sides.

2 Thread a 16-in. length of string through each hole and knot around the rim. Half fill the plastic bowl with water and float the ball in the water.

3 Ask a friend to pull the string on the ball toward him or her. There is now more water on one side of the ball. This is a tidal bulge.

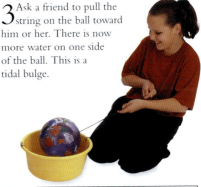

Pulling power

When the Moon and Sun line up at a Full Moon and a New Moon, their pulling power combines to create very high spring tides. A Half Moon means that the high tide will fall well below the highest tide mark. This is because the Sun and the Moon are at right angles to each other. Even though the Sun is farther away from Earth than the Moon, it is so big that its gravity still has a tidal effect. But at a Half Moon, they work against each other and create the very shallow neap tides.

4 The Moon pulls on the water as well as the Earth. So now ask the friend to hold the ball in place while both of you pull out the strings attached to the bowl until it distorts.

5 There is now a tidal bulge on each side of the world. One of you slowly turn the ball. Now you can see how, in effect, the tidal bulges move around the world as the world turns.

THE OCEANS' HIDDEN DEPTHS

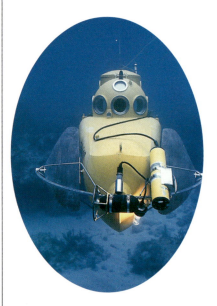

Nearly three-quarters of the world is under the oceans, lying an average of 12,238 feet underwater. In places, the oceans plunge down to a depth of 36,000 feet, which is enough to drown the world's highest mountain, Mount Everest, and leave more than a mile to spare. Seas cover four-fifths of the Southern Hemisphere, and three-fifths of the Northern Hemisphere. The five great oceans around the world are the Pacific, the Atlantic, the Indian, the Southern (around Antarctica) and the Arctic. The biggest of them by far (although they are all actually linked together) is the Pacific, which covers almost a third of the Earth. Until quite recently we knew little more about the ocean depths than about the surface of Mars. However, in the last 40 years, there have been remarkable voyages in submersible craft capable of plunging to ever greater depths, and extensive oceanographic (ocean mapping) surveys. These have revealed an undersea landscape as varied as the continents, with mountains, plains and valleys.

Probing the depths

Knowledge of the ocean depths has increased dramatically, thanks to small, titanium-skinned submersibles and robot ROVs (remote-operated vehicles). These can withstand the enormous pressure of 1¾ mi. of water above them. Satellites orbiting high above the Earth can make instant maps of the sea floor too. They pick up faint variations in the sea surface. These are created by changes in gravity, which in turn are caused by ups and downs in the ocean floor.

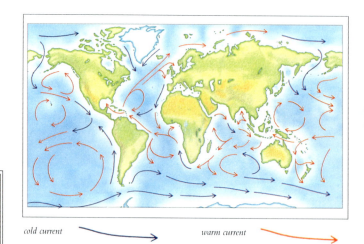

cold current ⟶   warm current ⟶

FACT BOX

- Seawater is 96.5% water and 3.5% salt. Most of the salt is sodium chloride (table salt).

- There are canyons under the sea as big as the Grand Canyon.

- The Mid-ocean Ridge is the world's longest mountain chain, winding 23,000 mi. under three oceans, including the Atlantic.

Currents on the ocean surface

The ocean waters are constantly circulating in currents. Those near the surface are driven along by the combined effect of winds and the Earth's rotation. They circulate in giant rings called gyres. In the Northern Hemisphere gyres flow clockwise, while in the Southern Hemisphere they flow counterclockwise. Deeper down, currents flow between the poles and the equator. These are driven by differences in the water density, which varies according to the temperature and how salty the water is.

Island rings

The Maldives are a series of atolls—ring-shaped islands of coral—in the Indian Ocean. The coral ring first began to form around the peak of a seabed volcano that poked up above the sea's surface. At some time, the seabed moved. The volcano moved with it and slowly sank beneath the waves. The coral, however, kept on growing upward, without its volcano center. The reef is sometimes hundreds of yards deep.

Coral reefs

Over millions of years huge colonies of tiny sea animals called coral polyps build reefs (ridges) just below the surface of the sea. As each polyp dies its skeleton becomes hard. Colorful living polyps live on the skeletons of dead ones, so gradually layers of polyps build up and the coral reef grows bigger. Coral reefs support an extraordinary variety of marine life.

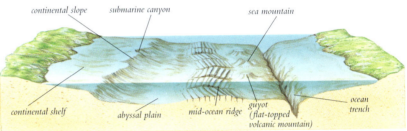

continental slope   *submarine canyon*   *sea mountain*

continental shelf   *abyssal plain*   *mid-ocean ridge*   *guyot (flat-topped volcanic mountain)*   *ocean trench*

The ocean floor

Running along the edges of each continent is a narrow shelf of shallow ocean barely 300 ft deep, called the continental shelf. Beyond, the ocean bed plunges down the continental slope into the depths of the ocean basin 6,500 ft below. The floor of the ocean basin is an almost flat plain, called the abyssal plain, which is covered with a thick slime called ooze.

Giant waves

The world's biggest waves occur in the biggest oceans, the Pacific and the Atlantic—and in the Southern Ocean around Antarctica. The more winds blow over the oceans, the bigger waves are likely to be. In the Southern Ocean, the winds roar around the world unhindered by land. Monster waves estimated to be 130 to 160 ft high—as high as an apartment building—have been spotted on occasion.

OCEANS ON THE MOVE

You will need: rectangular tub, pitcher, water, bathtub or inflatable wading pool.

THE OCEANS are very rarely completely still. Even on the calmest day, little ripples play across the surface, or the water gently undulates. When the weather is stormy, giant waves higher than a house can rear up and crash down, turning the sea into a raging turmoil.

Waves begin as the surface of the water is whipped up into little ripples by wind blowing across the surface. If the wind is strong enough and blows far enough, the ripples build up into waves. The stronger the wind and the longer the fetch (the farther they blow across the water), the bigger the waves become. In big oceans, the fetch is so huge that smooth, giant, regular waves called swells sweep across the surface, and waves may travel thousands of miles before they meet land.

Waves usually only affect the surface of the water. The water does move at a deeper level, in giant streams called ocean currents, if the wind blows again and again from the same direction. Some deep ocean currents, moved by differences in the water's saltiness or temperature, can stir up the water right down to the ocean bed. The first project shows how waves are made. Currents such as the ones in the second project happen in the oceans on a much larger scale, and circulations or gyres such as this swirl around all the world's major oceans.

MAKING WAVES

1 Place the tub on the floor or on a table. Choose a place where it does not matter if a little water spills. Fill the tub with water almost to the top.

2 Blow very gently on the surface of the water. You will see that the water begins to ripple where you blow on it. This is how waves are formed by air movement.

3 Fill the bathtub or pool with water. Blow gently along the length of the bathtub or pool. Blow at the same strength as in step 2, and from the same height above the water.

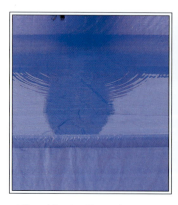

4 Keep blowing for a minute or so. Notice that the waves are bigger in the bath or pool, even though you are not blowing harder. This is because the fetch is bigger.

OCEAN CURRENTS

You will need: rectangular tub, pitcher, water, talcum powder.

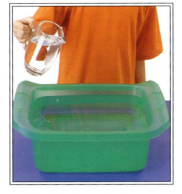

1 Place the tub on the floor or on a table. Choose a place where it does not matter if a little water spills. Fill the tub with water almost to the top.

2 Sprinkle a small amount of talcum powder on the water. Use just enough powder to make a very fine film on the surface. The less you use, the better.

Wind and spin

Waves in the Antarctic oceans are driven by the wind, ocean surface and the effect of the Earth's rotation. The main winds in the tropics, called trade winds, blow the waters westward along the equator, creating equatorial currents. When these currents run into continents, they are deflected, still warm, toward the poles by the Earth's rotation. Eventually, they run into westerly winds that blow the water back eastward again.

3 Blow very gently across the water from the center of one side of the bowl to the other. You will see how the water starts to move. Ocean currents begin to move in the same way.

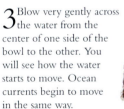

4 Keep blowing, and the powder will swirl in two circles as it hits the far side. This is what happens when currents hit continents. One current turns clockwise, the other turns counterclockwise.

THE WORLD'S WEATHER

STORMS, WINDS, snow, rain, sunshine and all the other things we call weather are simply changes in the air. Sometimes these changes can happen very suddenly. A warm sunny day can turn into a stormy one, bringing high winds and torrents of rain that then end just as abruptly as they began. In some places, such as in the tropics, on either side of the equator, there is very little difference in the weather from one day to another.

The planet's weather and every change in it is governed by the heat of the Sun. Winds stir up, for example, when the Sun heats some places more than others. This sets the air moving. Rain falls when air warmed by the Sun lifts moisture high enough for it to condense into big drops of water. On satellite photographs, swirls of cloud indicate how the air is moving. From them, meteorologists can identify distinct circulation patterns and weather systems, such as depressions and fronts, each of which brings a particular kind of weather.

The world's driest place
The Atacama Desert in Chile is the world's driest place, receiving little more than ½ in. of rain in a year. It is dry because winds blow in from the Pacific Ocean over cold coastal currents. The cold water cools the air so much that all the moisture in it condenses before it reaches the land. So, as it blows over the Atacama, it is very dry.

Antarctic cold
The coldest place in the world is Antarctica. In Vostok, the Russian research station in Antarctica, the temperature averages –72°F, and once dropped to –126.4°F. The Sun strikes polar regions at a low angle, not from directly overhead as it does at the equator, so its power is severely reduced. In winter, the Sun is below the horizon for most of the time, and it is night in the polar region for three icy months.

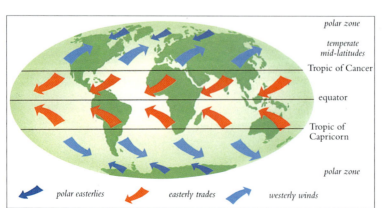

polar zone
temperate mid-latitudes
Tropic of Cancer
equator
Tropic of Capricorn
polar zone

polar easterlies   easterly trades   westerly winds

Winds of the world
Some winds are local, others blow only for a short while. Prevailing winds are those that blow for much of the year. The map shows the world's three major belts of prevailing winds. Trade winds blow between the Tropics of Cancer and Capricorn on either side of the equator. They are dry winds from the east. Moist westerlies from the west blow between the tropics and the polar regions. Icy polar easterlies blow around the North and South Poles.

Green and moist

The pasturelands of England are lush and green because they are well-watered by rain. England is in the westerly wind belt. Most of the winds blow in from the west over the Atlantic Ocean, where they pick up plenty of moisture that later falls as rain. Westerly winds also bring storms called depressions. These are places where winds spiral in toward a core of low pressure air. Depressions bring rain storms to the west coasts of Europe and North America as they move slowly east.

Perfect climate

Few places have such perfect weather as Quito in South America. It is close to the equator, so the air is warm, but because it is high up, it never becomes too warm. The temperature in Quito never drops below 46°F at night or rises above 72°F during the day. The weather is made even more perfect by the fact that just 100 mm of rain falls each month. It is no wonder, then, that the city of Quito is called the "Land of Eternal Spring."

FACT BOX

• The wettest place in the world is Tutunendo in Colombia, where the rainfall averages 460 in. in a year.

• The hottest place is Dallol in Ethiopia, where it averages 94°F in the shade.

• The place with the most extreme weather is Yakutsk in Siberia. Here winters can be -83.2°F and summers 102°F.

Monsoon rains

For six months of the year, some parts of the tropics, such as India, are parched dry. Then, suddenly, torrential monsoon rains arrive, as the summer Sun heats the land. Air warmed by the land rises, and cool, moist air from the sea is drawn in underneath. This rain-bearing air pushes inland. Showers of heavy rain pour down during the wet season. Then, after about six months, the land cools and the winds reverse and blow out to sea. Immediately, the rain eases and the dry season is back.

CLIMATE CHANGE

Storms warn of global warming

Extra warmth from global warming puts extra energy into the air, bringing storms as well as warmer weather. The industrial world pumps huge amounts of gases into the air, including carbon dioxide from burning oil in cars and power stations. These greenhouse gases are so called because they trap the Sun's heat in the atmosphere like the glass in a greenhouse.

EIGHTEEN THOUSAND years ago, the world was bitterly cold. A third of the planet was covered by thick sheets of ice. Vast glaciers spread over much of Europe and pushed far south into North America. This was just the most recent Ice Age. In the future, there will be another. The world's climate changes constantly, becoming warmer or colder from one year to the next, by the century or over thousands of years. These changes may be caused by a shift in the Earth's position relative to the Sun, or by bursts of sunspot activity in the Sun. Natural events such as volcanic eruptions, the impact of meteorites, and the movement of continents, also affect the weather. Recently, scientists have been concerned by the sudden warming of the world, triggered by air pollution.

Sunspot storms

Sunspots are dark spots on the Sun where the surface is less hot. They seem to change constantly and reach a peak every 11 years or so. Measurements from the Nimbus-9 satellite show that the Sun gives the Earth less heat when there are fewer sunspots. Weather records show that when they reach their maximum level, the weather on Earth is warmer and stormier. The next sunspot maximum is in the year 2002.

Ice core

A scientist investigates a core of solid ice that provides a remarkable record of climate change. The polar ice caps were built up over hundreds of thousands of years. Scientists drill into the ice of Greenland and Antarctica, and extract ice cores that are made up of layers of snow that have fallen over the years. They can detect changes in the atmosphere from microscopic bubbles of ancient air trapped within the ice and see how greenhouse gases have increased.

Polar ice caps

During Ice Ages, the Earth becomes so cold that the polar ice caps grow to cover nearby continents with vast sheets of ice. Ice Ages are periods of time lasting for millions of years. There have been four in the last billion years. During an Ice Age, the weather varies from cold to warm over thousands of years, and the ice comes and goes. There have been 17 glacials (cold periods) and interglacials (warmer periods) in the last 1.6 million years.

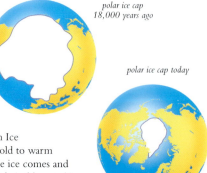

polar ice cap 18,000 years ago

polar ice cap today

Moving land

Everywhere on Earth has had a very different climate at some point in history. Fossils show that New York was once a desert, and icy Antarctica once enjoyed a tropical climate. This fossil is of a tropical fern, but it was found in Spitsbergen, which is well inside the Arctic Circle. Corals only survive in warm seas, but strangely have been found in cold, northern seas. Such dramatic differences are not due to changes in the global climate but because the continents have drifted around the globe.

Antarctic ice

The amount of ice in the world is always fluctuating. Antarctica contains 95 percent of the world's ice and snow. But even Antarctica has not always been covered in ice. In fact, most Antarctic ice is less than ten million years old. Icicles form as the warmer weather comes and the ice begins to melt.

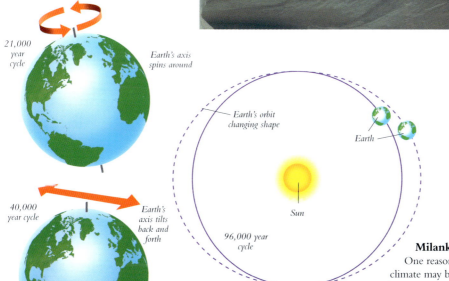

21,000 year cycle

Earth's axis spins around

Earth's orbit changing shape

Earth

40,000 year cycle

Earth's axis tilts back and forth

Sun

96,000 year cycle

Milankovitch cycles

One reason for changes in climate may be regular changes in Earth's orientation to the Sun. These are called Milankovitch cycles, after the Croatian scientist who discovered them. One cycle is the way Earth's axis spins like a top every 21,000 years. Another is the way its axis tilts like a rolling ship every 40,000 years. A third is the way its orbit gets stretched more or less oval every 96,000 years. All these changes affect how sunlight strikes the Earth—and so may have a dramatic effect on its climate.

WEATHER RECORD

CLIMATE IS the word used to describe the typical weather of a place at a particular time. The world's climates have changed throughout history. There have been times in the periods between Ice Ages, for example, when some plants and animals that are found in hot lands today lived in more northerly regions than they do now.

We can see how the climate has changed by studying weather records that have been made by people in the past, but these rarely go back more than 200 years. Scientists can also find many clues to climate changes in nature. In the sediments of sand and mud on ocean-beds, for example, they found fossils of tiny shellfish called *Globorotalia*, which coils to the left in cold water and to the right in warm water. By figuring out when the sediments were laid down, the scientists could discover whether the water was warm or cold by the way the shellfish were lying.

Ancient wood
You may find a fallen or freshly sawn tree in a forest to study. Scientists can take a record from a living tree by drilling out a small rod through the tree with a device called an increment borer. This gives a detailed record of climate changes Studying the past through tree rings is called dendrochronology, from the Greek words *dendron* (tree) and *chronos* (time).

This project shows how to make your own discoveries about recent climate change by looking at the year-by-year record of tree growth that is preserved in wood.

THE WOODEN WEATHER RECORD

You will need: *newly cut log, decorator's paintbrush, ruler with millimeter measurements, metric graph paper, pencil, calculator.*

1 Ask a tree surgeon or a sawmill for a newly cut slice of log. Use the paintbrush to brush off the dust and dirt from the slice of wood.

2 When the log slice is clean, examine it closely. Look at the pattern of rings. They are small in the center and get bigger and bigger toward the outer edge of the log.

FACT BOX

• Each ring in the tree's cross-section represents a year's growth.

• The strong line at the edge of each ring marks the time in winter when growth stops.

• A wide ring indicates a warm summer with good growth.

• A narrow ring indicates a cool summer with poor growth.

• See if you can spot good summers and bad.

3 Each ring is a year's growth. So count the rings out from the center carefully. This tells you how old the tree is. If there are 105 rings, for example, the tree is 105 years old.

4 Using a ruler, measure the width of each ring. Start from the center and work outward. Ask a friend to write down the widths as you call them out.

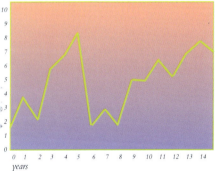

0 1 2 3 4 5 6 7 8 9 10 11 12 13 14
years

Long-term calendar
All kinds of trees are useful for tree ring analysis, though the sequoias (redwoods) and pines of California are especially valued because some trees are over 4,000 years old. By comparing rings from different trees, scientists can build up a record of climate change.

5 On graph paper, mark the years along the bottom line, using five small squares for each year. Mark widths for the rings up the side of the paper, using five small squares for each millimeter. Now, starting with year one on the left, plot your measurements as dots for each year across the graph.

6 Connect the dots with a pencil line. This line shows how the weather has changed with each year. If the line is going up, the weather was warmer. If the line falls, the weather was colder. See if you can spot if it is getting warmer or colder over time.

VEGETATION ZONES

S OME PLANTS, such as alpine grasses, can survive in very cold conditions, even if they are covered with thick snow for several months. Others, such as cacti, can cope with extreme heat. Each kind of plant thrives under particular conditions of soil and climate. Some groups of plants are so well adapted to conditions that exist in a particular region of the world that they are identified with those regions. The world can therefore be split into plant or vegetation regions according to the kind of plants that thrive there. Climate is the biggest influence on the kind of plants that grow, so vegetation regions tend to coincide with regions that have particular climates, such as tropical (near the equator), or polar (near the poles). Many different plants live in each place, and within these broad regions, conditions can vary enormously.

Barren tundra
Only lichens, mosses, hardy grasses and tiny shrubs such as dwarf willows and birches grow in the tundra wastelands. In these polar regions, the temperature rarely rises above freezing, and then only in a few months of the year. Plants must survive on little or no water in winter because it is frozen. Then, when the ice melts in spring, they have to cope with ground that is completely waterlogged.

Northern forests
Across the north of Russia and Canada are vast coniferous forests. These vegetation zones are called boreal forests or taigas. Winters are dark and cold, with thick snow. Conifers have thin, needle-like leaves that resist the cold, and snow falls easily off the cone-shaped trees.

Temperate grassland
Vast areas of the temperate zone, between the tropics and the poles, are covered with grass. Some of this has been created by farmers, as they have cleared woods for pasture, but much is natural. Temperate grassland is called by different names in different parts of the world, such as steppe in Asia and prairie in North America. Steppes are dry, so the grass is very short and coarse. Prairies are damper and the grass is lusher and longer.

Mixed woodland
In temperate regions, where summers are warm and quite moist, but winters are cool, the native vegetation is deciduous woodland. Deciduous trees lose their leaves in autumn. This reduces the need for water in winter, when frozen ground limits the water supply. Much of Europe and North America was once covered by vast deciduous woods, but over the centuries trees have been cut down or burned to make way for farmland.

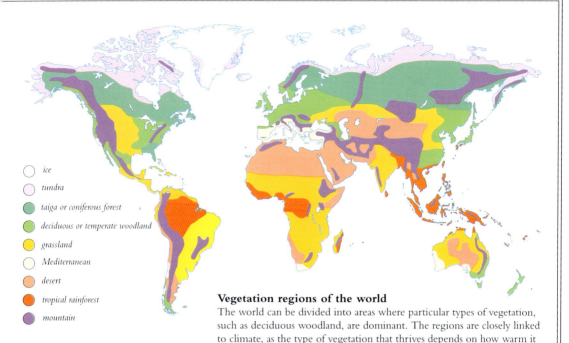

- ○ ice
- ○ tundra
- ○ taiga or coniferous forest
- ○ deciduous or temperate woodland
- ○ grassland
- ○ Mediterranean
- ○ desert
- ○ tropical rainforest
- ○ mountain

Vegetation regions of the world

The world can be divided into areas where particular types of vegetation, such as deciduous woodland, are dominant. The regions are closely linked to climate, as the type of vegetation that thrives depends on how warm it is or whether there is rain throughout the year or only in particular seasons. As the climate becomes colder away from the equator toward the poles (and higher up mountains), there are fewer different types of plants.

Tropical rainforest

Warmth and plentiful rain throughout the year make tropical rainforests the richest plant habitats on Earth. Deciduous woods rarely have more than a dozen tree species, but tropical rainforests may have 100 or more in a single hectare. The forests are surprisingly fragile because trees and soil are dependent on each other for survival. If trees are cut down, soil and the nourishing things it contains are quickly washed away.

Tropical grassland

Where rain in the tropics is seasonal, trees are rare, as they cannot cope with the long dry season. The typical vegetation is grassland, which in Africa is called savanna. Grasses in savanna lands grow tall and stiff. Dark evergreen trees such as acacias survive because their waxy leaves retain water, and their thorns protect them from animals in search of moisture.

THE BALANCE OF LIFE

Life on Earth may be classified into thousands of ecosystems. These are communities of living things that interact with each other and with their surroundings. An ecosystem can be anything from a piece of rotting wood to a huge swamp, but all the living things within it depend on each other.

Each living thing also has its own favorite place where factors such as temperature and moisture are just right. Some species can survive in a variety of habitats, but many can cope only with one. In an ecosystem, organisms depend on each other, and taking away just one species can threaten the existence of the others. If the plants on which a certain caterpillar feeds are destroyed, for example, the caterpillar dies, the birds feeding on the caterpillar starve and the foxes that feed on the birds go hungry, too.

Underwater richness
Coral reefs are the rainforests of the oceans. They provide shelter and food for an enormous range of marine plants and animals, from tiny coral polyps to giant clams and vicious predators. It is a fierce battle for life, food and space, however, and each species must develop its own program for survival. Even the starfish and seasquirts in this picture are predators.

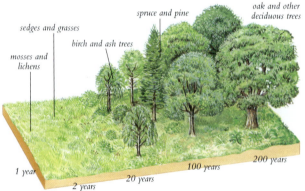

oak and other deciduous trees
spruce and pine
sedges and grasses
birch and ash trees
mosses and lichens
1 year
2 years
20 years
100 years
200 years

A succession of plants
When there is enough warmth and moisture on a piece of bare, rocky land, the first plants will grow. These will be the smallest, simplest plants, such as mosses and lichens, then tough grasses, that do not need very much to live on. The plants begin to hold the soil together. As they die and rot, they add nutrients to the soil, preparing it for bigger plants to grow. Soon there is enough to support small shrubs and tough trees such as pines, and eventually deciduous trees such as the oaks. This process is called vegetation succession, and it takes about 200 years for deciduous woodland to develop from the moss and lichen stage.

Harvest time
Farmland such as this has destroyed the natural vegetation and ecosystems. The number of plant species has dramatically reduced. A forest with hundreds of different plants may have been cleared to make way for a single crop. Because farming interrupts the flow of nutrients between soil and plants, the soils quickly become depleted, and farmers add artificial fertilizers.

Feeding habits

All animals depend on other living things for food and form part of an endless chain. This picture shows how the food chain, or web, works. A grasshopper eats a leaf, a thrush may eat the grasshopper and a kestrel may eat the thrush. When the kestrel dies and falls to the ground, bacteria break its body down and add nutrients to the soil so that new plants can grow. Herbivores eat only plants. Carnivores are meat eaters, and omnivores eat both vegetable and plant matter. Plants and algae make their own food from sunlight, and so are called autotrophs (self-feeders).

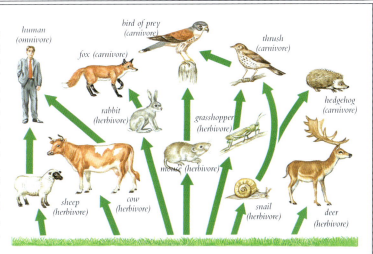

human (omnivore)

bird of prey (carnivore)

thrush (carnivore)

fox (carnivore)

hedgehog (carnivore)

rabbit (herbivore)

grasshopper (herbivore)

mouse (herbivore)

sheep (herbivore)

cow (herbivore)

snail (herbivore)

deer (herbivore)

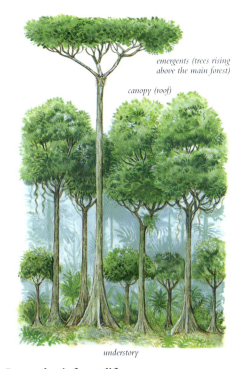

emergents (trees rising above the main forest)

canopy (roof)

understory

Layered rainforest life

Different types of plant and animals inhabit different levels of the tropical forest. Isolated trees shoot up to emerge above the dense, leafy roof of the main forest. Some are 200 ft tall. Below is a dense canopy of leaves and branches on top of tall, straight trees, 100–160 ft tall. In the gloomy understory beneath, young trees and shrubs grow and clinging lianas (climbing plants) wind their way up the trees.

A wealth of natural life

Swamps, ponds and all the other places known together as wetlands, were once seen as useless land that could not be farmed or built on. More than half the wetlands in the United States have been drained in the last 100 years or so. However, wetlands are remarkably rich environments, producing up to eight times as much plant matter as the average wheat field. They can also play an important role in controlling floods and are a valuable source of water in times of drought.

FACT BOX

• Tropical rainforests cover less than 8 percent of the Earth's land surface.

• They make up half of the world's growing wood and provide a home for 40 percent of plant and animal species.

LIVING TOGETHER

THE WHOLE living world is a vast and everchanging puzzle of plant and animal life. Each organism that is part of this living puzzle links or interacts with other living things, either directly or indirectly. The whole picture is so huge and complicated that even for scientists, it is difficult to understand how it all works together all at once.

To make sense of it all, ecologists often break the living world down into lots of smaller units, such as tropical rainforests or freshwater lakes. Then they might break it down further into smaller regions, such as a mountain slope. They might go further still to identify individual trees or a pool on a rocky seashore. Each of these units, where the things living there interact with each other, is called an ecosystem. One way in which plant and animal life interacts is through their food chain, which show what eats what in an ecosystem. Warmth and shelter and protection from predators are other ways in which plants and animals can benefit from each other by co-existing in an ecosystem.

Arrested life
The axolotl from the lakes near Mexico City never grows up into a tiger salamander. It stays a tadpole all its life. This is because the water it lives in lacks iodine, the vital ingredient to make it grow. If the axolotl is given iodine injections, it turns into a tiger salamander. But that would alter the whole balance of life in the lakes. This shows how delicate the relationship is between each living thing and its environment.

MAKING YOUR OWN AQUARIUM ECOSYSTEM

You will need: *gravel, net, plastic bowl, water, pitcher, glass aquarium, rocks and lumps of old wood, water plants, pitcher full of pondwater, water animals.*

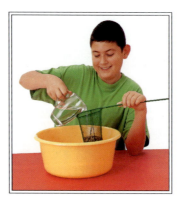

1 Put the gravel in a net and rinse in a plastic bowl of water or run it under the coldwater in the sink. This will discourage the formation of green algae.

2 Spread the gravel unevenly on the base of the tank to a depth of about 1¼ in. Add rocks and pieces of wood. These provide surfaces for the snails to feed on.

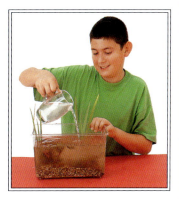

3 Fill the tank to about the halfway mark with tap water. Pour the water gently from a pitcher to avoid disturbing the landscape and churning up the gravel.

4 Add some water plants from an pet store. Keep some of them in their pots, but take the others out gently. Then root them in the gravel.

5 Now add a pitcher full of pondwater. This will contain organisms such as *daphnia* (water fleas), which add to the life of your aquarium.

6 Now add a few water animals you have collected from local ponds, such as tadpoles in frog spawn or water snails. Take care not to overcrowd the aquarium.

Specialized living

This giant turtle lives on the Galapagos Islands. It was here that the ecologist Charles Darwin noticed how island plants and animals adapt to their local environment in quite distinctive ways because they are isolated. Although the turtles originally had no natural enemies, they are now threatened with extinction.

7 Place the tank in a reasonably bright light, but not in direct sunlight. You can watch the plants in the tank grow. Keep the water clean by removing dead matter from the gravel every 6 weeks.

HUMAN IMPACT

From forest to wasteland
A hillside that was once rich tropical forest has been slashed, burned and bulldozed. Vast areas of rainforest are being destroyed, in Brazil and Indonesia especially, to provide wood and to clear the land for rearing cattle. Unprotected soil soon turns to dust in the tropical Sun, and farmers move on to wreak destruction on fresh forest.

HUMANS NOW dominate the Earth to a greater extent than any other species of animal has ever done before. The Earth seems to be in grave danger of suffering irreparable harm from our activities. The demands that humans make on the planet so that they can feed themselves and live in comfort damage the atmosphere, the Earth itself and plant and animal life. Car exhaust and factory chimneys choke the air with pollution. Gases from supersonic jets and refrigerator factories make holes in the atmosphere's protective ozone layer. Rivers are poisoned by agricultural and industrial chemicals. Unique species of plants and animals vanish forever as their habitats are destroyed. Forests are felled, vast areas of countryside are buried under concrete and beautiful marine environments are destroyed by tourism and sea traffic. The problem is not new, but as the pace of economic development increases, it is becoming more and more urgent to halt the destruction.

Poisoned air
Cars, factories and homes pour fumes into the atmosphere and are making the air increasingly poisonous to humans and plants. Lead has been eliminated in car fuels because of the damage it was causing to children's brains, and other substances may be responsible for a rise in lung diseases. Burning fossil fuels add sulfur dioxide to the water vapor in the air and cause acid rain, which pollutes lakes and kills trees, like these on Smokey Mountain.

Deadly algae bloom
A choked and lifeless river such as this is common. Few rivers in the world are entirely free from pollution. Of 78 rivers tested in China, 54 were badly polluted with sewage and factory waste. In Europe, most rivers have high levels of nitrates and phosphates from chemical fertilizers washed off farmland. Heavily manured land can make nearby streams so rich in organic matter that algae multiplies and chokes all other life.

Lifesaver
The rosy periwinkle is a tiny plant native to Madagascar. It was found to contain a chemical that has raised the chances of children surviving leukemia from 10 to 95 percent, by preventing cell division. Each hour, about 2,400 hectares of the world's rainforests are destroyed. Much will include precious plants like this whose value we will never know.

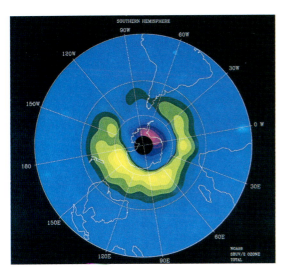

Destroying natural sunblock

The yellow and green blob on this satellite image of Antarctica is a huge hole in the ozone layer. Life on Earth depends on tiny amounts of the gas ozone in the stratosphere, 7½ to 31 mi. above the Earth. The ozone layer is our natural sunblock, and without it we have nothing to shield us from deadly ultraviolet (UV) rays from the Sun. This ozone hole reappears every spring, at both poles, each time getting bigger and staying for longer.

Exhaust fumes

Motor-vehicle exhaust discharges a wide range of unpleasant chemicals. Unburned hydrocarbons (better known as soot) make everything dirty and can cause breathing problems, while carbon dioxide adds to the greenhouse effect. Secondary pollutants are formed when exhaust mixes in the air. The worst of these may be ozone. This is a good sunblock in the atmosphere, but dangerous when inhaled. Soot reacts with sunlight and causes ozone-thick smog.

Endangered

The snow leopard is just one of millions of animal and plant species threatened with extinction by hunting or loss of natural habitat. Many species became extinct naturally, as the climate changed or a food source ran out. Today the rate of extinction is 400 times faster than the all-time average, all due to human interference.

The greenhouse effect

Carbon dioxide in the air is important because it helps to trap warmth from the Sun, like the panes of glass in a greenhouse. In the past, this greenhouse effect has kept the Earth nicely warm. However, burning fossil fuels such as coal and oil have increased levels of carbon dioxide dramatically, and this is collecting around the Earth. Vital waves of heat radiated from the Sun can filter through this layer to warm the Earth. But heat waves generated on Earth are becoming trapped. They hit the carbon dioxide barrier and bounce back again. This is making the Earth warmer. Experts think temperatures will go up 39°F in the next 100 years, bringing extremes of weather, rising sea levels and flooding.

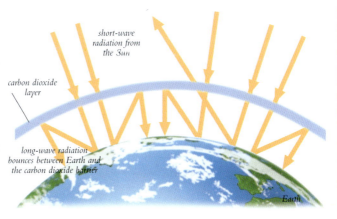

short-wave radiation from the Sun

carbon dioxide layer

long-wave radiation bounces between Earth and the carbon dioxide barrier

Earth

DANCE OF THE CONTINENTS

ONE OF the most amazing scientific discoveries of the 1900s was the idea of continental drift. Scientists discovered that the world's continents are not set in one place but are drifting slowly around the world—sometimes meeting, sometimes breaking apart. Recent high-precision measurements by satellite show that the continents are moving even now at between ¾ and 8 inches a year—about the pace of a fingernail growing. This may seem slow, but over the hundreds of millions of years of Earth's history, the continents have moved huge distances. There are ancient magnetic rocks within them that are like frozen compasses. Scientists can use them to plot how the alignment of the rocks has changed, and how the continents have twisted and turned. Piecing together these and other clues has gradually revealed just how the continents have moved over the last 750 million years.

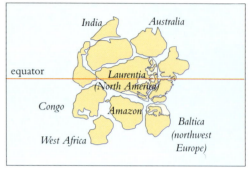

700 million years ago (mya)
All the continents are welded together in one giant continent that today's geologists call Rodinia. There are none of the recognizable shapes of today's continents. Magnetic clues in the rocks confirm that North America lay at the continent's heart along the equator and northwest Europe to the south.

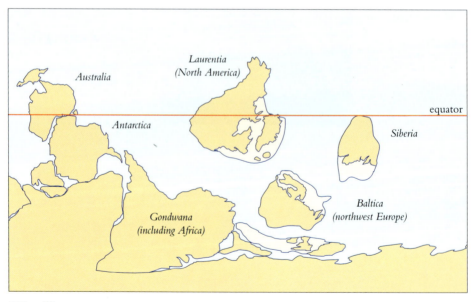

500 million years ago
The simple continent of Rodinia has broken up, but some of the fragments have gathered again around the South Pole. The map projection exaggerates the size of this South Pole continent, called Gondwanaland, but it was still massive, including all of today's Antarctica, Australia, South America, Africa and India.

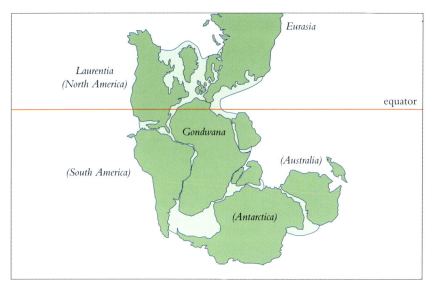

250 million years ago
Gondwanaland has merged with Laurentia and all the other continental fragments. A single mega-continent has formed and sits astride the equator. Geologists call this super-continent, Pangea (all earth). Pangea was surrounded by a single ocean, which geologists call Panthalassa (all sea). 200 mya, soon after the dinosaurs first appeared on Earth, Pangea began to break up.

50 million years ago
Between 200 and 50 mya, Pangea slowly broke up. First the Tethys Sea between Eurasia and Africa was opened up. Then the land split apart between Africa and South America to open into the South Atlantic ocean. By 50 mya, North America had drifted away from Europe to open up the North Atlantic. India was powering north into southern Asia. Australia was out on its own.

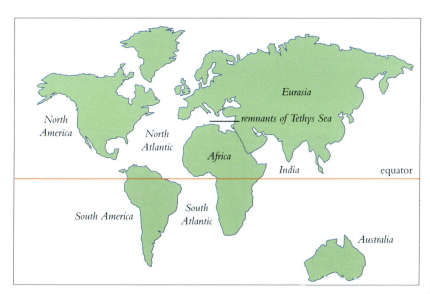

The world today
The continents today look familiar and set. But they are moving even now. In another 100 million years time the map of the world will look very, very different. The Americas are moving so far west that they will probably bump into eastern Asia in time, obliterating the Pacific. Africa will split into two parts and its eastern side will drift into southern Asia. As for the rest of Earth, only time will tell.

GLOSSARY

abyssal plain
The broad plain across the lowest level of the sea bed, up to 16,400 feet down and covered in ooze.

acid rain
All rain is slightly acidic, but when pollution by sulfur dioxide and nitrogen dioxide reacts in sunlight with oxygen and moisture in the air, it creates acid rain.

alluvial
Anything to do with sand and silt deposited by rivers. An alluvial plain is built up from silt deposited by a river.

anticline
An arched upfold in layers of rock.

archebacteria
A very ancient form of bacteria able to survive in extreme conditions, for example in scalding volcanic waters in black smokers on the sea floor. They may have been the first lifeforms on Earth.

arete
A sharp, knife-edge ridge between two mountain glaciers.

atmosphere
The blanket of gases surrounding the Earth.

atoll
A ring-shaped coral island created as the reef round a volcanic peak goes on growing at sea level while the volcano sinks beneath the waves.

aurora
Spectacular displays of colored lights in the night sky above the North and South Poles.

barchan
Crescent-shaped dune in a sandy desert.

base level
The lowest level a river can wear down to—usually sea level.

berghschrund
A deep crevasse at the head of a glacier made as the ice pulls away from the valley side.

biome
A community of plants and animals adapted to similar conditions over large regions of the world. Sometimes called major life zones.

black smoker
Chimneys on the sea floor that belch black fumes of superheated water.

cirque
A deep hollow in mountains carved out by the head of a glacier.

continental crust
The thick part of the Earth's crust under continents.

continental drift
The generally accepted theory that continents move slowly around the world.

continental shelf
The zone of shallow water in the oceans around the edge of continents.

convection
The rising of hot air or fluid because it is lighter than its surroundings.

core
The dense, hot metallic center of the Earth.

crevasse
A deep crack, typically in the surface of a glacier.

crust
The solid outer shell of the Earth, varying from 3 to 50 miles thick.

cycle of erosion
The idea that landscapes are worn down, through youth, maturity and old age, again and again.

denudation
The gradual wearing away of the landscape.

ecosystem
A community of living things interacting with each other and their surroundings.

erg
A large sea of sand in the desert.

erosion
The gradual wearing away of the land by weathering and agents of erosion such as rivers, glaciers, wind and waves.

fault
A fracture in rock where one block of rock slides past another.

fetch
The distance winds blow over the sea to create waves.

firn
Snow compacted into ice by melting and refreezing.

glacial drift
All the material deposited by a glacier or ice sheet.

glaciation
The molding of the landscape by glaciers and ice sheets.

greenhouse effect
The way certain gases in the atmosphere trap the Sun's heat like the panes of glass in a greenhouse.

guyot
A flat-topped mountain under the sea, typically a volcano that has been eroded at the summit by waves, and which has then been submerged.

hanging valley
A side valley cut off and left hanging by a glacier.

hot spot
A place where hot plumes of molten rock in the Earth's mantle burn through the Earth's crust to create volcanoes.

ice age
A long cold period when huge areas of the Earth are covered by ice sheets.

igneous rock
One of three main types of rock, created as hot molten rock from the Earth's interior cools and solidifies.

joint
A fracture in rock between blocks that have not moved relative to each other.

lava
Hot molten rock emerging through volcanoes, known as magma when underground.

lithosphere
The rigid outer shell of the Earth, including the crust and the rigid upper part of the mantle.

magma
Hot molten rock in the Earth's interior. It is known as lava when it emerges on the surface of the Earth.

metamorphic rock
Rock created by the alteration of other rocks by heat or pressure.

mid-ocean ridge
A long jagged ridge on the sea floor along the gap between two tectonic plates which are moving apart.

moraine
Sand and gravel deposited in piles by a glacier or ice sheet.

nappe
A complex mass of folded-over rock strata in mountain regions.

orogeny
A major period during which fold mountains were formed.

ozone
A form of oxygen gas. It is poisonous, but a layer high in the stratosphere protects us from the Sun's harmful ultraviolet radiation. The ozone hole is where the ozone in the stratosphere is very sparse.

Pangea
A megacontinent of about 220 million years ago that divided to form all today's continents.

permafrost
Permanently frozen ground, in which temperatures below 32°F for more than two years.

plate
See tectonic plate.

rift valley
A valley formed when a strip of land drops between two faults.

strata
Layers of sedimentary rock

stratosphere
The layer of atmosphere above the troposphere where temperatures climb higher with height.

subduction
The bending down of a tectonic plate beneath another as they collide.

syncline
A dish-like downfold in layers of rock.

tectonic plate
The 20 or so giant slabs of rock that make up the Earth's surface.

thermosphere
The layer of the atmosphere above the mesosphere, beginning 50 miles up.

till
Mixture of rock debris left by an ice sheet over a wide area as it retreats.

tor
A clump of big blocks of bare rock on top of a smooth hilltop.

transverse dune
A dune at right angles to the wind.

troposphere
The lowest layer of the atmosphere up to 7½ miles.

weathering
The breakdown of rock when exposed to the weather.

INDEX